PRAISE and THRENODY

BY ROBERT HAZEL

Poetry

Poems, 1951–1961
American Elegies
Who Touches This
Soft Coal
Clock of Clay

Novels

The Lost Year
A Field of People
Early Spring

PRAISE and THRENODY

ROBERT HAZEL
COLLECTED POEMS

CIRCLING RIVERS
RICHMOND, VIRGINIA

CIRCLING RIVERS

PO Box 8291
Richmond, VA 23226 USA

CirclingRivers.com

ISBN 978-1-939530-15-8 (paper)
Library of Congress Control Number: 2021930542

ISBN: 978-1-939530-16-5 (hardcover)
Library of Congress Control Number: 2021931228

Cover art: "Ceremony at Dawn," by Jean Huets

To Robert Hazel's friends

CONTENTS

CEREMONIES (IV)

CEREMONIES (V)

FOREWORD

*Hart Crane pouring back into the language, and behind him Walt
Whitman, the main current flowing, but gracefully; the natural, special,
endlessly ambitious American poetics; the true inheritance.*
— Barry Spacks on Robert Hazel

POETS, AMONG ALL kinds of writers, adhere most to lineage. If a poet
loves Walt Whitman, he won't mind old Walt looming "behind him"; if
she loves Hart Crane, she's fine with Hart Crane "pouring back into the
language" via her work. Novelists and essayists tend to name influential
books. Most poets, like musicians, cite their teachers, however obscure,
and even troublesome, with reverence and pride.

Poems themselves, though, adhere to no line, horizontal or vertical,
national, stylistic, or chronological. Heaped all together, poems act more
like compost. Their diversity—broken twig and shattered leaf, turd and
scrap, worm and grit—enriches each other and us.

For all of poetry's riches, and despite a few collections that spring
from social media onto bestseller lists, people don't read poems much.
Leaves of Grass never realized for Walt Whitman his dream of being
America's bard—not during his life, maybe not even yet. If a nation's
bard is a poet whose work and persona deep-weave into the identity of
that nation, America might not be cut out to have a bard. Compare our
Nobel-crowned rock-and-roll star Bob Dylan to Shakespeare—not the
quality of their work, but what they are and will be to their nations. Maybe
America is too diverse, her identity not coherent enough, to support a bard.

As Walt Whitman discovered on acting as his own publisher, poetry
rarely brings profit. University presses are (barely, tenuously) subsidized.
Big publishers absorb the loss as prestige. Small presses pray not to go
broke. Even if a publisher snags a poet who gives knockout readings, wins
prizes, and garners praise from powerful critics, publishing poetry by and
large remains a "passion project."

Circling Rivers, a publisher of poetry and literary nonfiction, is a
small press—a very small press. Our issue of this collection by a dead and
never prominent (though highly praised) poet is surely a folly and will not
answer any prayers connected with money or fame.

Several factors prompted me. (Me, as in, the editor. My partner is the
business manager. There. That's our staff.)

Robert was my poetry teacher in college, and of all the teachers I've had in school, he's the one I most admired and the one who helped me most.

There's the lineage, yes, that too: the lineage of American poetry. Letting Robert Hazel's poems disappear would rupture it.

The most compelling reason for publishing this collection, though, is that Robert's work remains powerful and relevant today, decades after he wrote it, and even more urgent. As James Dickey put it: "Reading Robert Hazel is like having a lost limb restored: one that comes back full of joyous and ruthless power."

Wendell Berry describes/interprets Robert's aspirations, and captures what Robert could achieve: "He wanted a fabric of imagery and sound so dense and so tightly woven as to be impermeable to prose." Berry cites "Celebration Above Summer":

> *Hear dark the priestly insects of my endless summer*
> * coast down to cells of wax,*
> *and kind weeds bend my flowers to their colors' end...*

A poem like "Celebration" can read chaotic as an overgrown vacant lot in high summer, chaotic as a disintegrating love affair, chaotic as poetry can be.

Barry Spacks found in such language a weak point, "a distracting, distancing showiness." Some charged that the brilliance of the words over-dazzle their own meaning, that the poems' effects outshine the poems themselves. I'm with Robert Buttel, who wrote, "Hazel's post-symbolist, surreal poems ... are the most haunting, brilliant, dramatic, and compelling, as well as the most baffling and resistant. It is these poems that demand the most scrutiny and offer the greatest rewards." These concentrated poems offer fragments that the imaginative reader must make whole, or leave as irreconcilable. It's pretty much like life, like America, like love.

This is not to sentimentalize. Robert's poetry is not designed to offer comfort; its beauty isn't pretty. Robert Bly could almost be accused of understatement in saying, "He dislikes the usual clean-shaven version of American history." That was before American history grew stubble. Bly foresaw that Robert's poems would echo the cries of America decades later.

The poem "Who Touches This" is more plain-spoken than works like "Celebration Above Summer"; it allows prose to permeate. Its prophecy sings in the lament of an inebriated (hence, to Robert, perhaps that much more visionary) lone man, sieved through the waking dream of a poet:

The lone black man
in this gritty precinct of flower children
woke me at 4:00 this morning
crying, "Whore of Babylon!"
Near sleep I heard something
perfect as a dream
so certain that I felt
it would survive my waking
It was only the hoarse
repetitions of a drunk man
shouting, cursing, weeping
how this nation was killing
all his innocent children
Yet strangely when he stood
pounding the garbage cans
and imploring, "America!"
the word sounded beautiful
as if he believed it…

Robert cries out as if he believes, like Walt Whitman but without Whitman's determined optimism, that poetry can make his country sweet and whole, ideal. But his American heroes are those slain in violence: John F. Kennedy, Malcolm X. And his and our America is too much made of bucolic decay and urban blight.

Robert cries out, too, in love, as if outrage can purge romance of betrayal and imperfection, as if beautiful words can build an earthly paradise—all the while knowing it's but a beau geste.

Robert titled one of his poems, and one of his collections, "Who Touches This," drawing from Whitman: "Who touches this, touches a man." Not a person, not every man or any man: a man, in all his pettiness and glory.

Robert exposed wounded masculinity and observed, acutely and with outraged compassion, wounded femininity: what happens when in hope or need of love or gain of some kind, the body is given, or taken, then exploited, and its bearer, girl or woman, discarded or kept for further manipulations.

"Ode to Teenies of Tompkins Square" initially read to me as the pout of an aging man-child. *Nailed to the cold green benches / hurt-hearted girls spitting semen...* But a less defended look reveals more. Like their twirking celebrity surrogates, the "teenies" on the "cold green benches" are jiggled, jingled, and trained to entertain, their sexuality reduced to dismal "benefits." Men fare no better; faceless, they're cocks to be jacked. "Ode" provokes and offends; a few lines of it are nearly laughable. But its indigestible truth cannot be denied.

Walt Whitman contended in his way with the sacrilege of the body electric in the name of patriotism, when he nursed soldiers shredded by our nation's rage against itself during our Civil War. "Teenies" gives witness to the desecrations we wreak on each other in the name of love and self-gratification.

The lover in Robert's poems can be vengeful, vicious and raging. At times, he's merely a bawdy buffoon. He can be, too, tender, gentle, at times almost fatherly, at times doglike, servile.

He doesn't forget joy, though love brings only moments of ease. "Green Girl" expresses happiness, shame, lust, boastfulness, contentment, wonder, grief—all that passion can inflict, in images meltingly lovely and earthy raw.

> *I let my head fall back full in joy*
> *My bones genuflected to her spine*
> *I gave her an apple smile for her cider,*
> *   for her joined and jointed body*
> *   like a petal puzzle*
> *   all yellow as tobacco...*

"Green Girl" has, too, that composted quality; within it are poems Robert showed me: John Crowe Ransom's "Bells for John Whiteside's Daughter," Theodore Roethke's "I Knew a Woman," Dylan Thomas's "Fern Hill," the heart and voice of Federico Garcia Lorca.

DESPITE ROBERT'S CAPACITY for great tenderness, Wendell Berry's correspondence with me leaves no doubt that Robert's equal capacity for wreaking emotional havoc left a bitter trail at University of Kentucky, where Berry was his student in the 1950s. Robert, with his beautiful young wife, cut a dashing figure on campus, but his penchant for self-destruction scarred those close to him, including his soon-to-be ex-wife and his then-young student Berry.

I met Robert at Virginia Tech, twenty years on. He was, probably, wiser and mellowed, though another of my writing teachers there, Bill

White, described his beloved friend as "a heathen, a rascal, an urchin child of the earth." As an earnest young poet, I was shocked not by Robert's excessive drinking but by a sign he had on the wall behind his desk, there for all the world to see: "Way down deep, we're all pretty shallow." Really? I asked him. He smiled, shrugged.

Heathen, rascal, urchin he could well have been, and shallow we all may be, but Robert was deeply read in poetry. He showed us, his students, the way of poetry: the writing of it, and the reading of it. He wasn't prolific in terms of published work, and some of his published poems are, frankly, crap, yet poetry was for him no spare-time occupation. "In poetry," he said, "I get close to what I really am."

As Robert's student, as a poet, as a person, by him I felt cherished. Never did he make me feel ridiculous or shamed, though I made a fool of myself a few times in his company (we all drank at his parties), and I wrote my share of sophomoric poems. We corresponded after I left Tech. I'd send poems, and he'd return them with keen, sometimes impishly humorous, and always helpful comments. For all the carelessness he subjected himself to, Robert took care of us. He wrote me once—I don't remember why; who knows what happened to the letters I wrote to him—"You know that Robert Hazel won't let you go hungry or cold." For all the despair he poured into his work, he possessed a noble urge to encourage others. He wrote, answering what must have been a gloomy letter from me: "In this world total cheer is not possible, but be as optimistic as you can. Because I care, Robert."

Frances Whyatt, another of Robert's students and a friend to the end, wrote: "He was a great poet, and a great man. He believed in the supremacy of love and nature. He was generous with his time, money, friendship, talent, and abilities as a teacher and guide to his students certainly, but also to the farmers who lived nearby his place in North Carolina, to the old Italian ladies in his neighborhood on Sullivan Street, and even in his troubled and often tragic love life."

Robert's attentive care extended, like Walt Whitman's, especially to the refused. Unlike Walt, he often counted himself among the refused, tumbling into both self-pity and genuine despair. From "Sunday": *Loss is my skill / Let every man be perfect at something.*

Again like Walt Whitman, he never presumed to speak for the underdogs of his time. We never lose the boundary between observer (poet) and observed. But when Robert sees his people, we see them, and he doesn't let us look away. From "Heads Up":

the cinders of Sunday black girls in a Birmingham church,

the corpses of white girls whose fear-wet flesh was a threat
to the National Guard of Ohio…

In some ways, Robert seems almost to want to undo the work of his poetic ancestor Walt Whitman, even as he connects with it. Walt tried to ennoble America by embracing her, the rough with the smooth. Embrace the America of Robert's poems and you'll bleed.

Toward nature, Robert is more forgiving. His and Whitman's outdoors is always human-touched. "Celebration Above Summer" brings us to a farm, not a wilderness.

> *O see my land turn back,*
> *my summer pond waved with cattle, my ironweed candelabra*
> *burning,*
> *my knotted chickens, sure claws austerely clamped and*
> *dawn-triggered…*

Robert's "Who Touches This" quotes "So Long," one of Whitman's final poems—not final chronologically, but final as Walt wished it, placed toward the end of his life's work *Leaves of Grass*. In Whitman's "So Long," poetry gives way to the personal, the physical; the tempestuous sorcerer gives way to the man:

> *My songs cease—I abandon them;*
> *From behind the screen where I hid I advance personally, solely to you.*
> *Camerado! This is no book;*
> *Who touches this, touches a man;*
> *(Is it night? Are we here alone?)*
> *It is I you hold, and who holds you;*
> *I spring from the pages into your arms—decease calls me forth.*

ROBERT—ROBERT ELVIN HAZEL—WAS born on a farm near Bloomington, Indiana, on June 27, 1921, the oldest of three boys and one girl. His father was an assistant professor in physics at Indiana University and co-authored *Physics: A Basic Science*, a standard high school textbook. His mother was a homemaker.

The family moved to Ashland, Kentucky, when Robert was seventeen. There, his father helped found New Ashland Junior College (now Ashland Community and Technical College). It was as a student there, according to Robert's brother Herbert, that Robert's "interest in literature really kindled and subsequently his great love for writing and poetry." Robert left home to serve three years in the Marine Corps. He got his undergraduate degree at George Washington University and his Masters in 1952 at Johns Hopkins University, where he studied under poet Karl Shapiro, and met his friend Louis D. Rubin, Jr., who published some of Robert's early poetry and went on to found Algonquin Books.

MA in hand, he headed to New York City, where he got a job as a book editor. In 1955, he joined the faculty at University of Kentucky as a creative writing teacher. John Barth summed up Robert's career there: "The University of Kentucky, not everywhere regarded as a seedbed of American writing, once turned out a surprising clutch of notable literary alumni, including the poet Wendell Berry and the short-story teller Bobbie Ann Mason [and James Baker Hall, Gurney Norman, and Rita Mae Brown], all coached by the poet and novelist Robert Hazel who dwelt some seasons there."

Robert had two novels and several short stories published in his thirties, but it wasn't until he was forty that his first collection of poetry was published. In 1962 he left UK, briefly taught at Oregon State University, then moved back to New York City, where he taught at NYU and in 1972 was poetry editor at *The Nation*. After he left New York, he lived for several years at a red farmhouse, in western North Carolina. He taught at Virginia Tech from 1974 to 1979.

He retired to Eustis Lake, Florida, close to several members of his family, including his mother, whom his friend Bill White, who also lived near Robert, described as a "remarkable lady." In his early 70s, health problems, especially skin cancer and heart disease, escalated. He died of suicide in 1993, leaving a note: "Dear Family, / Not drinking. Not sad. Four days and nights of physical torture without relief killed me. / Love, Robert."

This "just the facts" timeline leaves out the disastrous womanizing that bounced Robert out of at least two teaching jobs and in and out of five marriages, the drinking that tore apart his career and his marriages, and the bitter sadness—what could be diagnosed, I suppose, as depression—that tore apart himself, once a boychild he called "honey Robert me." It leaves out, too, his unquenchable and "inimitable joie de vivre," as his friend Frances Whyatt said, and his generosity to students and colleagues, family and neighbors, his genuine care that commanded an enduring loyalty from those—like Whyatt, and Bill White, and Linda Kandel Kuehl and John Kuehl, who stuck with him, though he didn't always make it easy to be his friend. (I took the liberty of dedicating Robert's collection to his friends.) It doesn't touch, either, his ability as a teacher and clear-eyed mentor to fire a devotion to what he taught us: poetry, fiction, and the writing of it. Most of all, a biographical sketch of Robert cannot capture the chiaroscuro joy, even ecstasy, expressed in his poems.

WHEN I KNEW Robert, I was too young, too full of my young life, to see what his more mature friends saw, that his adult life was a long, alcoholic slide down. Some pin his poetry to that trajectory—not implying it deteriorated along with him; it didn't. They see it move from bright potential to nihilistic despair. From what may be his last poem, "Clock of Clay":

> *I am becoming nothing.*

Life, and Robert himself, did heap on the man sorrow and physical malaise. His poems allow no escape from human cruelty, ignorance, bigotry, loneliness, bereavement, waste. D.H. Lawrence's exasperated charge against Walt Whitman's work can be stuck (albeit out of context) to Robert's work, and to his ideals of love: "It always slides into death." Yet Robert continued to love, he honored love, he believed in love. From "Clock of Clay":

> *Love, Thou, at once / Love, Thou, excessively.*

Robert Hazel's shaken faith pervades his work; his experiences saturate its images and tones; his sins and virtues brought it forth. In themselves, though, the poems no longer match their maker's life. Our physical bodies may be "clocks of clay," but poems have a possibility of cutting loose, living beyond our times with other poems that have outlived their makers, living through chaos and furious love, living in us, their evergreen readers.

— Jean Huets
Richmond, Virginia
September 2020

PRAISE and THRENODY

CEREMONIES (I)

CEREMONY AT DAWN

Dark leaves foal a white moon
unguided by running clocks in the tin town;
the stones are buried that marked the land's thin sections
    and dialed the sun;

in that country my fathers and their brown women
    clamored with birds at dawn
and chewed oak leaves for the chorused mouths of children
    bright on a pasture of mares;
windlasses of light hauled up the sun
    in buckets from the clear sluices
and wheat flooded with light the insistent stones
and children bandied grain in a white turning
under the water that purified the stones
and washed wild moonrings from the eyes of mares
that all became gentle and kissed the bit,
and children played under the mares' tarred feet;

west a field of sedges leans to re-enter the knowing earth;
north the wind shakes a squirrel tree's barking snag
and hollow bole full of young musk sweetening the wind;
a meadow of ironweed tarnishes the moon's climb south;
east where my fathers worshiped a young dying god
a chapel of shingles settles in a stillness of bells;
the tombs on the hill spool fine spiders and ferns;
immaculate bones turned salt are licked by wild mares
    so many days hand-running to devour,
their skulls are stones in the certitude of water
and ligatures of ash return the larch;

now lodestones of still earth at dawn charm
my fathers braiding ropes to haul the sun

up from the dead fern ocean
and light their chaliced eyes that saw the land grow green
under the claybank mares that rode their caskets hard—
they shake incense of blood on furious leaves!
I wear a veined oak leaf honeyed with tar
where rushing hooves brush with black mayhem,
and my skeleton like a fish in coal;
the neighing of mares reared on the threshing floor
and the stone chimneys bolted with iron stars
guide now with mercy all my lost children
in the very whitest day of my knowing.

PRODIGAL

PRODIGAL

Holy, my corrupt beast near breath
I lead by leather to your unending death,
kill, and you walk quietly to be
drawn and loved at my blue knee,
its patience on gravels, its next stony pain
your next of killed kin,
come in random drives of new dust
where my land is beaten thin, its crust
a green tidings that also dies
close to the packed roots and the lies
of water, if water could speak
through its narrow stone beak,
cry in dead gullies, drive merciless green, still
with murderous trees and brigand grass, come to kill
with my knife-handed start
toward you, round there like my own heart,
holy beast! carved, craved by days, crimes, friends, if they were
able to follow you, come insistently to wear
my leather out, dragging you across frozen Christmas
into sodden Easter when snow on the grass
cannot let loose, even ice not wanting to die
at long length tapered from green roofs, try
to stay fixed to each zero of my mind
where we, lashed together, find
deep dust by flashlight in tin barns, come knee-deep in blood
to your sold shipped slipping death, endless, red,
holy, draw nearer, now see
high birds with round eyes, their easy sickle over my blue knee.

THE PINCHED FACE OF VIRTUE

A correct parlor, a correct wall-clock, a 60-watt light
    corrected by a plastic shade
& the sofa dustless & on a dustless end-table
    the Standard Revised *Bible*

Suddenly my father's bloodless face, legacy of privation
    & endless correction

PRAISES

Corn tassels, pig bristles, pond water, wave me;
sun in the black twigs, father me warm;
call burlap mists to rise, and the sky,
chaste in a clearness of dead stars,
to float my rusted nails and barbed wire coils
where the day's high tatters hang in the breath
of dead orchards with snow eyes
and my ardent father's love-murderous disguises
austerely cold in laurel,
more destitute than singing masks cut in white stone;

O see me dressed in a bright shirt as I,
crucifer at the head of a cortege
of my several corpses, go
while beside me the flat-sided sun bumps on the road
and sunflowers roil their ripenesses my eyes train
on the corymb of remembered candlesticks:
wax and char of my endless lovers and abandons:
polish the flanks of my swift mirages,
ring in water laments of my holy flesh
and the crick in my ribs that is proud of disease;

father, the brown girls in your tall house whisper
and the bleating of your slaughterhouse comes to my ear
a sweet tirade spoken by a girl of high color
and the rings on my homemade hands glow red in a shower
        of lamb's blood
and miniature suns parade in the small perfect faces
        of their hardness;

by day, by night I see you always in a spectrum of praise
while here the milky dog-day sky hurrahs buzzards
and rains mud beyond the beak-reach of vigorous birds
        to oil and preen
and my head is drenched with choiring wet butterflies.

CORNUCOPIA

Wings of insects deaf in time,
scrape the cross-grained falls of my birds'
and animals' quick whistles and pardons
from brittle twigs, not strong enough for nesting
and late leaping in thin tandem sprouts
and soured grapes, gums, barks, and the last straw
that shouts the presence of surprised eggs
     broken to no Easter,

carve the yellow air, skein my clear earth
with careful webs, thin enough for breaking
    across the new winter of my eyes,
                cry your small being
at my strewn gates of new gifts and silences
among blue-shouldered calves and doves.

ELEGY FOR WILLIAM

> *... that as this never*
> *again shall bear*
> *Green leaves or branches, nor increase*
> *with any growth his size;*
> *Nor did since first it left the hills and had*
> *his faculties*
> *And ornaments bereft with iron ...*
>
>   — Iliad

Scented and plumed, this handful of earth
that heard the inrushing breath
and stood up in a green husk to walk
ore-drunk and light-blind on the land
falls from the broken hand that held its manshape
    in creation;
the hand is an empty furrow pointing at crows;
I follow, guided by woods odors tawnier than applemeat,
to measure and dig an acorn's grave, tended by spiders;

when William passes on the trestle of his coffin
    adrift in cut flowers,
I would not stop him; I would not slow the going
    of one who laughs as he rides by;

I think of the voyages great trees make on the water,
    their branches white with salt;
shut in that sensual river, I have seen
his timely shape bottled in green rain
on bell-leafed trees beside the slow canals,
drawn by gingerly mules to a delta
    of shattered miracles;
there a child stood mouth-deep in the quickness of women
who wept and prayed Christ for love's taint and savor,
my breath was sodden with many kisses and prayers;

after I dug the grave, I came down from the crows' parapets
to the public market where the posts hung full of rabbits,
and came through the odors of baking loaves on the tongues
    of pestles
to touch the ornamental hands in the coffin,
curled like cockfeet frozen in white weather,
the ticking barn vane telling the wind how it blows,
how William's body gathers a harvest of women,
green-sheened stalkers moving excellently
in torrents of unfelt flowers and glass beads;
counting and counting, the women sift his dust,
auguring the potency of talismans;
how old men lean on sticks to the coffin's gape
    at their dry leather,
no February water in eyes that weave the amity of death
a tapestry fat with quail at hunters' belts,
the wind in strands, and they accustomed to the scald
    and reek of entrails;

autumn is new, heavy, but undesiring
as the leather and flax it wears;
autumn turns the women's hands brown,
their eyes red with suffering;
those dun-colored women by the linen wind

feel bells burn lichens of the womb;
they chafe in the security of madonnas;
women with stone feet and gaze turned salt
feel cold bronze crowing in steeples
above the wild oats that toughen their hands;
and birds, cried up by the bells in their flaming yolks,
dip rings around a dark instinct that signals
the feather lofted north from Capricorn,
and under them, gray claws folded, the bells wave
brown sedge and loud oat to ripe weaving evening
and cover him with ground-running vines;
his corpse is paved with leaves and vinegar,
furnished with pots of corn and ironweed spears,
his blood dried black and sweet;

at nightfall, under drifting hair, children suck and dream
    the confirmation of huge blossoms;
they are not scattered separate on hillsides
where their milkless fathers rave wordless
claims of green privilege from the earth
    that falls against the sea,
from trees that seine the moon out of the sky;
they are untorn; unborn, they lie in no manger of myth
nor is any star burst to dry their watery ears,
nor is any love while pity kisses their curls,
nor wise men come with snorting beasts to anoint them
whose dreams echo, tongues clamor and cry
to an earth of high maize, staminas, strides, bells, praises;

when to let the young fall in birth—that is spring;
the script of harrows shall record their birth;
cut sod shall drum them early with blinded eyes,
yet by morning the land shall have no injury
    to show a birdsong;
all silver minerals preening to black shall be
thronged sugar and wax and green paint on a stalk
    mounted by garrulous tassels;
the stalk in its vestments of the reveling east,
and they shall feed and fable and bray triumphant summer;

sometimes we inhabited stones where crows whet their beaks
and foxes ran shrieking like orderly girls;
he, an old man, hung a water-gourd on a sunflower
        in the presence of clouds
and the earth grew fat with his libations and tumors;
I, a child, braided the incredible hair of angels
        and applauded carrion
from the high advantage of crows with my round eyes
while his laughter grew a tall tree in my ear,
        controlling the shapes of birds;
and I heard his laughter at fairs and carnivals
until the wheels stopped turning and the barkers declared
        nothing huge and improbable in darkness,
whiskey, tobacco, candy dried on his mouth;

foxes show themselves on the hill,
        their shapes bold,
beckoning toward the oxhorned ravines;
now to this country of cirrus bells and barking star
a white mule fed on Easter's bloom comes;
King of Mules, he brings once more to William
the green-thighed woman who caused his blood to shout
swift as spellbound goats paw and cry;
she feels him drowse in horror of dogs and crows;
she watches the dying beast come from his hide to trample
the castles of ants that dig for the noise of his tongue;
his jaw locks in a bond of soil and blood;
to his lips spring thin flowers with iron-purple leaves,
and she who sewed with red yarn ravels love;

I have inhabited my father's shape forever;
he has not shown me the earth;
his rib is not yet caved to create the woman
        in whose sweet body I shall lie,
who shall wear me on her fingers;
he is in a still country;
a green hood covers my father;
neither evil nor good can come to him,
        chanting the barbarous sun;
no word has yet been spoken to create the woman

in whose sweet body I shall lie,
whom my father shall wear on his fingers;
good and evil walk round
my father's green hood in fear;
neither evil nor good can come mourning
    the leprous moon to my father
whose love despises all things pure.

CATAFALQUE

As I grow young and new
I forget sound and light,
radios and rainbows
traffic lights bend
over streets in rain,
the loud drop of tinfoil
on plazas in New York,
the hail of weed seed
on sod in Indiana.

I grow new into silence,
I keep only the deaf,
hanged by white wires
that run to invisible ears,
the crippled with candle legs
in the sanctuary of steel braces,
priests in brown robes,
sandaled in snow,
rabbis in white stockings
closing the Sabbath
across tin cans and cyclone fences,
arms held like broken wings.

I hold deafness and blindness.
I lead myself
into new silence.
For the first time I see
my young wife's face,

the silent symmetry
of her blind eyes.
I have never seen
even in an apple
or a cadaver
so much beauty.

New things grow as I grow
and fall into silence.
I do not know anything
except dictionaries and catalogues
I read as a boy
in my sheepskin coat,
barricaded with rifles
in my green and cindery country,
in cornfields and steeltowns
dressed up with people
who were all beautiful.

I keep the deaf
trapper of foxes
whose dumb hands
fled away at dusk,
and the girl who never
saw a mirror.

This is my nature:
to guess stones and flowers
before they rot and seed
the wind its random motion.

I cannot remember
when I grew young and younger.
When I was twelve, my father
gave me a dictionary
so I would know
what I mean.
I will never know.
To know would be unlike me.
To inherit blindness and deafness
I teach myself.

I keep for fields and cities
a plain map that I drew
from memory in grammar school,
with mountains in brown,
lowlands in green.

My geography is simple.
I lead myself here
by a red wrist
into the captivity
of bright October sun.

In my new greed,
I lead myself to the stone
steps of a gray building
under the clock tower
of a university.

Beside this temporary scaffold
of books, maps, leaves,
boys and girls pass,
carrying books and candy.
I have never seen
even in broken bottles
and varnished crutches
so much beauty
as their quick legs and skulls.

This is the braille
of my lost vision.   My country
is raised and shallow.   My country
is red and yellow.   I wear
its coat of many-colored lies.
In my hands, without fingerprints,
I keep this dust to quicken
a new death.
                              Bells strike
over New York and Indiana,
an hour wide.   Hearing the time

announced in bronze,
I go past a hardware store
with white blocks of salt
out front.   I go, among students,
carrying each other's hands,
without a word, and blind.

POOR ROBERT'S ALMANAC / BURLESQUE

When I Heard the Learned Astronomer

When I heard the learned astronomer
pinpoint the city & how to bomb her,
I hid my head amid a cloud of mosquitoes

The Drunk Carpenter

Don't nail the walls up tonight
just because you feel skillful & sweet

Not striking the head of the nail
would be sinful

Your hammer is true temper
forged by your mother

Going Away

I thought I wore a suit but didn't
The wrinkles didn't match

It was a party
We were invited downstairs for a drink

I spoke to a friend & was fired from the job
My estranged wife sailed on the still lake called Atlantic

How do you form the weld between the coke & the beer cans?
Say them in the voice of your first kiss

Frailty

I found the Siamese cat whose owner was a little Florida
pompom-headed football girl who was interested only in copulation
& had left this place for the stiffer tongs of Daytona Beach

I discovered the cat, all ribs & fur, almost too weak to walk,
giving suck to four kittens

I knifed off a fillet of raw fish I'd just caught
After giving me her blue-eyed thanks
the cat ate & ate & ate delicately

A little girl came downstairs to watch.
I asked who feeds the cat?
Nobody, she explained, you don't have to
because the mother cat doesn't give the kittens food
only milk

Free Lecture, Public Invited

Sartre died today, condemned by the Church

In the St. Johns River in Florida green fish leap

Energy upsets

Go lightly, Holly, thru Africa

Muhammad Ali, I presume?

An E-flat minor chord with a sixth in the bass is C,
        E-flat, B-flat, C-minor, seventh flat-five

Verbs are my acts
Memory is know is meat is bone is cartilage is suet
Verbs cavort naked
From my life verbs escape into dream of whats   Yes,
& I tell me because nobody else listens

I drink to think
At nine I'm fine
If I break this habit, I'll die

Stick it, Black, Stick it, Black
into the universal White microphone

If God knows everything, I know it better   I am *here*

Failure is no accident   If I fail you, it's because I have red hair

Better the lie that glads you than a sad truth
Avoid psychology
Rejoice with mushrooms
Do not sweat in love-making

The mule is a trumpet
The banjo is a straw
The lover is when
The grass is true
The cradle is love

The Pope of I-81

I gave my papal blessing to all cars, vans & trucks on I-81

This is the traditional trace of the Cross
        across my forehead & level with the license plates
        of Maryland & Virginia, etc.

But while I blessed a Toyota Corolla
        in the right lane ahead
a filthy 14-wheeler from Tennessee hauling pigs
        cut in front of me & blew straw
        painfully into my left eye

Okay, while I gave The Finger to the sucker
I veered left & hit a Recreational Vehicle from Georgia
        carrying husband, wife & three children
Their vehicle careened across the median,
        rolled twice & all persons
        went up in flames

Fortunately I was unhurt & my car was not damaged
A man like me, with many social responsibilities
cannot pause to regret the fate of only five persons

Tribute to Camus

The depth of his wisdom
was the height of despair

People Try

People try hard to look nice
It's enough to make you cry

Humoresque

Dearest little Betty Maxson
I am on the train from Jackson-
ville to Richmond, Va., I love you

There were three long varnished boxes
with green wreaths and brass-bound corners
loaded on the West Coast Champion, too

We went walking through the park
goosing statues in the dark
Sherman's horse can take it, why can't you?

Passengers will please refrain
from flushing toilets while the train
is standing in the station, I love you.

Life in these United States

TAVARES	— A mother who believed she was the Virgin Mary and admitted drowning her little daughters in a bathtub was found innocent of murder by reason of insanity
TALLAHASSEE	— A convicted rapist had three years added to his sentence for "chronic masturbation," even though the Florida prison system has no rules against the act

TALLAHASSEE   — An attorney for convicted killer Ronald
                 Jackson argued his client shouldn't be executed
                 because he is retarded & he suffered brain
                 damage from sniffing transmission fluid

BALTIMORE   — A man who admitted killing his
                 girlfriend's 10-month-old son
                 by throwing him
                 down an 11-story trash chute
                 was released by an appellate court on
                 the grounds his confession was made
                 12 minutes too late

DETROIT   — Murder charges against a former high school
                 girl's basketball coach who confessed to killing
                 four prostitutes have been dismissed
                 by a Recorder's
                 Court judge who ruled
                 that police had violated the law
                 by holding the defendant too long for
                 questioning.

Brushing the Fish

In spring when the fish rush up the river ripple to spawn
we boys & girls break willows to brush the fish up to dry ground
& if a girl steps on a fish with her bare foot
she wins a kiss without having to read *The Golden Bough*.

Has To

To begin

I, being of unsound mind & sad,
am glad to start anywhere
& expect to lose this will
quicker than hair or
a fish with roe

No way

Me

Some way

Each morning she speaks with Christ
Each morning her daughter speaks with Christ
Nothing bad can happen:
murder, theft, arson? No. God wills so.
They are my mother & sister,
to whom no harm can come

Anti acid

For my nervous brother—
anti food, alcohol, love-making—
He's supposed to die without even trying

One time

We children brayed like mules
Our cheer voices shamed the wind
Myself age three I hear
My left eye takes photographs of
while my right stares at a loud child
Clock, wind down to our silent now

Three to make ready

But where to go?
Piss on the roses, light a cigar
& call it quits?

Wing nut

If you screw it too tight
you wring it off
& water spills all the rest of your life

Wait for it

Inspiration—all day I walked & went home without it
It shied away from the tangerine dandruff fell on

Needless to say

A lone man is happy in supermarkets
The aisles of vegetables
once I grew by the bushel
and jars of clear honey I sold in town

You tell me

Why poor men can't be cured of dreaming
Why the gods play possum
Why I try to touch these thoughts like rain

WHO TOUCHES THIS

to Walter Freeman

Every time I dream, I am alive
Every time I remember a dream,
I know I have lived

Mother, lie
Father, rise

I live in the mountains and work the farm
my father and I cleared and kept green
I hear a creek bubble loud like my heart
and thrushes' wings whisper over the hill
I meet my boyhood on a gravel road
and see how beautiful I was then
honey Robert me

Dreams! My skull explodes with dreams
like the white heads of dandelions
I sit in a room in Manhattan
hearing empty bottles fall,

savage words in other windows,
the gears of a garbage truck
I live in the pain of my father
who tried to cross his hands
when he choked and choked
when the last stroke struck

If I have no way to go
that way is good
I am learning how not to live
I shall forget every valuable thing
last and first forget the woman
I said love to said love said love

I will tell you a bitter thing, blind heart:
the wild ways you have perfected
the way hunters create the life of a deer with knives

The purpose of learning is to forget before you die
But a man must try to learn something unspeakable,
        something that makes him tremble

The lone black man
in this gritty precinct
of flower children
woke me at 4:00 this morning
crying, "Whore of Babylon!"
Near sleep I heard something
perfect as a dream
so certain that I felt
it would survive my waking
It was only the hoarse
repetitions of a drunk man
shouting, cursing, weeping
how this nation was killing
all his innocent children
Yet strangely when he stood
pounding the garbage cans
and imploring, "America!"
the word sounded beautiful
as if he believed it

I have become my face
My face smiles for me
on public occasions
when a man's peers
are all photographers
Then at 5:00 p.m.
I return to an old vacancy
called my heart
And where will you speak, Robert,
after 5:00 p.m., and to whom?
Tell a dimestore mirror
how you have loved
father & mother, brothers & sister
and a woman from Brooklyn?
God, drag these loves
at the end of a leather halter
like the dead cats and dogs
I dangled as a child
at the end of a dusty rope
before they begin to stink!

I have written this in a ring-binder
that belonged to a friend who cut his wrists
There is a smear of blood on the cover

It is nearing dawn
This is the way I say no to God
and the way God laughs back at me
in the cold shirt of my skin

COW SALT

for Henry Birnbaum

White the blocks stacked on the street
before a hardware store in Indiana, savory in the sun
Henry Birnbaum, *schön* as his peartree name,
asked what. I said, Cow salt.

He gave a New York weary shrug.
Cow salt? There's no such thing!

I bent & cradled the life-giver for
how many years of fertility—
O my rush deep into the green where
I set the salt!

I don't go anymore where it is hauled
stay miles & miles away from slaughter
It stalks me in dreams
Nor have I lately strolled on Avenue C
in New York City where Henry led   I fear
that little start to die

May I sit in your house, Hersh ben Simon, & see
on TV the Washington Redskins? And on
your walls all the books & paintings
Love is simple permission

Trailing no clouds of glory, we come...
our teachers dead: Whitehall & Cargill—
friends in the earth or rotting in silence
In this grim interim of breath
the beast-me whimpers, unslaked,
calling to an emotive runt
I have dragged experiences behind me
like a mean dog   It snaps
Surcharge on my spirit? Nobody here to pay
I'm not in society, but log hours haunted
in a womb of green ferns
I choose nothing   I'm untracked
Yet less love was laid on the line than mine
O I have been beautiful as October!
Who will pay the tax now on my blemishes?

And you, Henry, not your brain clean
as a nail nor often wisdom can
fence chaos at the border of your last haircut
Billy Kilmer could have told you better

or your father, mystic Simon, closing the Sabbath over
the East River
Reason?   Forget Spinoza & Kant
rare archaic intoxicant   How many sober mornings
have you died trying to imagine a prayer
you cannot utter?

White on the street, the blocks of your disbelief
Lot's wife looked back, too

If the salt shall lose its savor
who will remember the sting
to my cut hand, to your blind eye
the first pain of holy?

SILENCES

Childhood

I heard corn grow
I dented the moon with an air rifle

Nobody else in Indiana could do that!

My parents' god demanded suffering
Should I have tried another way?

An American child, I played a radio
so I'd not have to listen to music

Musicians don't understand silence

Magic is silence
silence smells like new shoes

Ancestry

Inheritor of Whitman, Hopkins, Crane
trousers, belt, shirt, socks & moonburn

Philosophy

Charles Dickens & James Wright excuse our crimes
Ivan Karamasov & I will never forgive us

Simone Weil said it: Humanity is one
of God's least successful experiments

I have friends whose stomachs are cut.
They are silent as sea turtles

If water will fall, let it
Water gives you no choice but silence

The Condition of the Culture

Intelligent conversation is lacking because
few understand the intricacies of football

Hamlet as quarterback & Ophelia as wide receiver
draws a blank at Radcliffe

But Shakespeare knew Columbus, Ohio
His mind was cleansed by that high terror

In New York City roaches picked
my teeth clean while I slept

Poverty

Good women stewed the broth of my troubles

What troubles?
I am only dying

In return I gave them all my money
They held me closest just before leaving

Ambition

To ride in triumph through Indianapolis
Unveil my limestone statue on Meridian!

Reply to Ambition

My favorite aunt: What *ever* will become of you!
Her favorite nephew: Nothing

Croquet

They're about to stake out
and I don't even have a position

Isolation

Other people do things
Why does nobody invite me?

What was love like?
The echo of minnows?

Goodbye, Poem

Why hang you on the line to dry?
I lick glue
It is the hoof of a dead horse

DELLA YOUNG TO THE POET

Well I was glad and happy when the mail came
I been wanting to write you a few words
but couldn't find your address That's my failing
never know what I do with anything
and put in hours searching and studying
But I have got so I like it Something to do
I set up till 1:00 a.m. till after midnight
I wrote a batch of letters Now you wonder
One to Bud and wife's boy in Germany
one to Bud and wife in California
married with four boys one in Germany
and another in Vietnam one retarded
and the least one still at home
One to Madonna that lives in Indianapolis
Madonna has one boy through high school

and a sick husband in the hospital
I must not forget her She and her husband
send me money all the time
for medicine and things to eat
I am not keeping roomers anymore
I pay the whole shebang lights water telephone
and all breakdowns like sewer stopped up
painting and papering The light system
went out Something wrong and cost $40.00
had to pay that but Madonna and husband paid half
We have had two deaths in the last two weeks
Luther got burned up in his own house That ain't
no way to do things I wished I could have told
poor Luther that ahead of time and saved the funeral
expenses Allen the funeral director got his new
funeral home finished it off with a green awning
just in time for Luther to burn up before his time
The first funeral was held It was a double deal
from the Legion and the Old Soldiers
Luther and a old man that stayed all night with him
years ago when they worked on the railroad
and ate beans from the same old black bucket
We have a new preacher Bro. Davis from Arkansas
He his wife and two little boys They come
up to me before Church began and talked to me
and made the little boys talk and call me Grandma
When they went away all around me
them little washed-up devils says who
Who was that old woman Sister Young?
I was that sister Young I said the new preacher family
they said they didn't know which one and I said Who?
I am who prayed here before you knew who
I was that old woman that knew Bill Hazel
and went out to pull the weeds off his grave
and I am who nursed Bill's boy Herbert when he was sick
and I am who took Bobby Hazel, Herbert's son, in hand
and taught him verses and spelling before you whoever
you are ever got up here to this country
so don't go asking me I felt ashamed for them
I said to them Well, if you want to get acquainted with somebody

write them a letter like I did
I had wrote the preacher and his wife soon as they come
They didn't even know I had a daughter named Madonna
Well Madonna's man's doctor said can't go much farther longer
He has diabetes Boils come out all over his body
Neither is Madonna She has ulcers Had all teeth pulled
$400.00 to get them out Don't know how many stitches
in the jaw But she got new glasses and can see again
I get choking spells sometimes Sometimes when it's bad
I don't even recognize Ed when the police call me to come
up there and take him out drunk Sometimes
when I think about it I take choking spells Sometimes
don't even know my own little brother Ed in the jail
Eddie is all the brother I have now He is very poorly
He has took to drink Eddie with his heart condition
He and his wife was drinking and she got mad at him
and broke his guitar that he had won the Nashville contest
with He shake his head He just cave in Eddie and was so mad
at her She broke his guitar right over her knee and throwed
the pieces against the wall She said Go get em and pluck em
one more damn time And shake his head and look at his prize
guitar like a batch of kindling for the fire
so finely He said all right I am leaving
I will just move out to the hen house
She said Good enough So he took some old clothes
and a skillet and some flour and a coffee pot
got him an old broke chair and set in the hen house two hours
it was getting dark the kids come a yelling in
and somebody knocked on the back door It was Ed
Said Can I borrow a little baking powder?
She shut the door in his face and laughed till she cried
the kids cried half scared and slinging snot
This is February 2nd and the groundhog seen his shadow
but I ain't worried about it It's cold with a deep snow
5 degrees below zero All water pipes froze
I have went to Services at Church every time
They had to slide me in the car with a shoe horn
All around me six widow women in a block of me
One old she-devil hard of hearing I can't talk to
That old deaf widow has a little fice dog named FDR
She watches the Television Can you beat that!

Hard times here The faucets all froze up
but I pray daily I wish you and all of yours
health happiness and God's Grace
This botched-up letter is like Bill Hazel used to say
Looks like somebody had written it hisself!
I love you all, all my dear kin and never saw any
of our tribe but what hadn't the same right to their name
Hard times here after all was gone, the girls, my husband
sick or dead or moved down to Florida or to California
But Bobby you didn't never forget to come and visit me
when you was in this part of the country
You come by and sat on the porch with me and jollied me
and reminded me when you was painting Luther's house
before Luther burned hisself up in the fire
how I had carried you up a gallon bucket of ice water.

OOLITIC

A small start in my lungs, infant gills waving
over graves under gravel, little boy,
toy of limestone water, afloat by chance over
fern under falling fish

Build me of bone-eye when I went swimming
in quarry water over trillions of fish skeletons
& my other brothers gasped clean up to the wet sky,
        tongues bobbing

& the girls' long bodies in cotton swimsuits shrinking
        faster than eels

Under the green water of natural sunken baptism & numb
        womb start to here from the history of fossils
        climb into time,
        spit, lick, stare & wonder
        why I'm no longer a seam in perfect stone

WILDLIFE

Softer than the insides of my woman's thighs, the calls
of owls mating on my pine mountains

Whitman's shy thrashers' evenings of wine, throbbing
from musty bottles

Chill nights possums gnawing the entrails of dead cows
Bright day, hear the jays arrogant as gods

When the otter grins his fangs in the lake
it's time to wonder more about dying

COUNTRY PICNIC

The concupiscence of girl voices
at touchdowns by boyfriends,
a hotdog, a touched breast

The murmur of my elders
facing death down with potato salad
& whispers of cancer

Children cracking walnuts with hammers,
their acrid fingers stained yellow

Myself carving faces on pumpkins
for little ones with happy candles
that drip deeper than they know
on sudden hot wrists,
their first flash of mortality
in cries of telltale burn

So I praise the virgins before
hard times set in
after wedding rings cure their giggles,
cold kitchens at morning & cries
of infants ill & dumb

& the boys who run with footballs,
craving praise, beer & pussy

& my elders at our reunion,
saying our names aloud
so God can check them off
among the sheep, not the goats

So I praise my nephews who light
charcoal to glow in their eyes

ANABASIS

> *Dangerously the summer burned*
> *(I had joined the entrainments of the wind).*
> *The shadows of boulders lengthened my back:*
> *In the bronze gongs of my cheeks*
> *The rain dried without odour.*
>
> — Hart Crane

Cumberland Gap

Overland my fathers leaped at my throat,
scrambled the blue shale of Virginia,
rode Cumberland Gap, protesting my image
in pools in the lap of tall rocks,
crosscreek into laurel and wild grapes they pursued me.

The checkerboard lowlands, red and black,
staged hoof and wheels' disconsolate play,
but they struggled, nothing could stop them
from the seizure of my image in darkness.
At last they got me past the thin line
of trees round death's black gaum,
shadowed from the midwife's red hands,
blazoned by firelight
in their wild eyes—

Little Darlin,
we'll carry you to Salt Lick where you'll see
Sandy Clauses reindeer come down to the crick.

I suck reindeer, Dear.
The yellow milk of peat and morning cobweb caters for me!
Goats, mountain lions, mule-deer
nudged in the short white hair.
Hushabye hushabye! Will give it a fig.

On Clear Creek

Take one gift for a life, the prickly flesh
that gored a proud man's heart
and lay above his woman's shaved loins
when I was blind and whole
spun a little melody in my gills,
song of a fledgling in undergrowth of time
that folds love's wing over the midnight face
of his inveterate crime.

Loose in beast-fable and folk-song,
I lied beyond my own believing a thing,
and I created earth's prosperity
and ate the bloom of a honeysuckle vine
and slew my thousand violets with a dog's hind leg.

Beyond science and law she wrestled my body
into a wilderness of light and shadow,
a level universe where planes of color
were caught like beasts in thickets of tapestry
until their forms, penitential and clean,
dived into her breast where I found
that roundness is most perfect in anything.

The moon was prisoner of my window frame
and rode my rivered skin
and because time is a four-fold logic
took an orbit of remembrance,
and I knew the evil of childhood was long.

Inheritor of wind and ores of the sun,
I have been caught with wildfowl and herbs in my teeth.
Differentiation is suffering—
stones ground smooth but men irregular
in drifts of singleness and cruel behavior—

shucked out of red-tasseled childhood by the second
of three rude hands, ignoring green,
hung to season and dry
in the menopause of philosophy,
in the smile of a worked-out woman.
I had no hair when I lived undersea.

The tortoise may become a bird with wings

Old Woman, bake a pie for your King of Heaven
    while breath and goodness consecrate a ring
put four and twenty blackbirds in a pie
    for death is the only enemy of grace
and serve a jolly dish to the King of Heaven
    and only the weak make preparation to die
a jolly dish to set before a King!

Cheraw Revisited

Sigmund Freud
raised the curtain on a mangled nude,
commanded greatness from the mouth of Joyce
and led Picasso to idle fantasy
in cheraw cheraw cheraw,
green wings in a gold garden
cheraw.

Plaster of Paris arms
and icy dorsal fins,
a breast in medical sections
and the eye blind with blood
disgorged and hanging by the optic nerve.

Wind me by three wishes, and like a toy,
set me one sure course across the rug,

the same direction that overtook the child,
feed the moist labials of impulse
that short the rational circuit of mind
so that I speak: Nofretete Nofretete,
maud pristine stalk of strawy love high
in tasseled chryso of libidinous riches
still wet and green—

                      I wearing shoes and hat
and waiting for the dream-producing state
wherein all crime is swallowed by desire
to fix the moment by its varnished wing.

I am an ornate jardiniere for storms
and yellow wild flowers drink in me
and float lilies of consciousness folding worms
above the surface of the Theban's blood.

I pressed a child's hand to a windowpane
and frost returned its burnt magnetic kiss;
spectrums eddied round each fingertip.

His hand was like a butterfly's wing,
a perfect gradual bloom of mindlessness.
He grew to incompletion and was lost,
and the black silk on my arm is a sunken dream.

I often grieved for goodness
but then I came upon myself again
in Vienna, Paris, Zurich, and Cheraw
in the evening of a system of law.
Two green and golden muvvas in Cheraw
sat in a private garden in Cheraw
diddling sweet afternoon away.

Desert Passage

World of the desert, silican cry of wind
careless as dust where it flies,
the vegetation pointing the wind's way

but they kept order; misdemeanors were few;
there was no reason to thieve while they kept together.

Tanyard bodies, glutted pores,
fed by desire that burned in long-flued furnaces;
they knew how to make the air draw
blue pupas of ember.

Now from that region come the best infantrymen,
those mannerly slow-smilers who strand the wind.

The long head of armor-plate,
moon hook of the beak in air.

Leather is on the wrist and heart, the falcon's subsidy;
the hush of their faces is the blazon of heralds

Chieftains walk the badlands of their eyes,
lay about with sticks, cry up the birds
in smoke of treble wings, halloo from sight
all fear and fury in long cones of repose
and the trampled bush rises and points at the wind.

They ate small game and drank the water of plants
while rain shied from them
and the weed rolled in their throats
and the sun's torch
rang on hair and bone and cortex.

You are astonished at their dialects,
blue songs, green dances,
their women like rifle slings sighting them in
the black notch and bead of their destruction.
You are astonished at their suffering.

Thales, pray for Einstein.
Anaximenes, pray for him.
Heraclitus, pray for him who is astonished at suffering.

Leucippus, Democritus, Lucretius, pray for Einstein.
All atomists, pray for him who is sick.
Aristotle, pray for him.

Pythagoras, Atreya, Aristarchus, pray for Einstein.
All holy researchers, pray for him who has no commission
    from Hell or Heaven.

Straon, Eudoxus, Hipparchus, pray for him.

Poseidonius, pray for him.
Berossus, pray for him.
Ptolemy, pray for him.

All spearmen who went with Philip and Alexander,
you who ate green corn with Cyrus in Persia,
you who followed Hannibal out of Africa,
all pray for Einstein who is sick of suffering.

Starry tongues of Babylonia and Chaldea
pray for him
when the desert entreats you
when mirages suggest to you
ideas of correspondence between the stars and men.

All holy angels, lift him down from their eyes.

King of the Hill

Sunrays in the darkest houses
seep dry crystals, seek their common level,
mercurial mirrors whose frozen surf ripples the wall

brightens the eyes of sorrowful carolers
with frostbitten hands and spiny hair
of the white boar.
Arthritic ash trees and rheumy willows—
pensioners awaiting mandible and saw.

Take the goblet of ice, cherry red carolers
for you must entertain the ur-season.
Leave the skin of your tongues on a slick tree or an axe
and go self-wronged to the guilty wedding.
Marry the patient ones to gilt eggs of fish
whose skeletons launch stone.

The weakness is uniformity: trees all bow down;
holly-berry noses daze a wreath;
the river perch gasp one song,
drumming beneath ice till the quicksilver thaw,
the mirrors turn black and run.

Lot's Gardens

Possessed by charity and regaled in the plumage of love
I would banner the sky with goodness
and flame the immaculate east
with all pure colors of my blessedness,
and I would not look back on Lot's gardens
to see their trellises yawn smoke and salt,
for what is uglier than a broken heart?
who more miserly than a beggar in the street?

Would angels have charity to steal my wings while I slept?
restoring my crooked bones and fallible marrow
and the hope of grace for sake of only ten men
who lie in beds of gaudy grass and wreaths?

It is not wax I am scorching,
It is the heart and spleen of Lot I scorch.
It is not I who bury him in the hills
far from the beloved city.
It is Gabriel who is burying him.

Dynamo

A dynamo is singing.
The black core whirs, cuts the field
of the real and imaginary.
The black cat purrs, of time
a reliquary.

Light is an eye at the tip of copper nerves,
aphrodisiac of houses and barns.
The women discard their lamps—
oil, tallow, wicks.

Addison's spacious firmament
burns to an unfixed point.

Tomorrow cleaves the egg before the sperm's
hard journey into yesterday could yield.
Children only have yellow eyes to anoint
and the cock crows before Peter can ready
his midnight heart.

The Virgin of Pittsburgh

White water from those hills fell
into the black city. It was good for that
and good to sit in the crags of its headwaters,
sensing the caprice of engineering—

here the nighthawk, a scrawl on the sky,
there the red star, a rag doll dancing;
the city below is a chorale to the glory of
a girl with small bones and a narrow pelvis,
with eyes blind as pearl and as beautiful

Tomes of odors swarmed the traps and basins,
rose from wet cobblestones of memory
to the boarded windows, caved her nostrils
in upon the glued fine hair, and she cried for the water
that rinses memory from the lace of moments
covering her body, and looking at herself, bemused,
    when I look exactly like myself
    the scar upon my abdomen is pleased
smiling
I shall never take a man upon me,
a ram, a dog, a cockerel, a pony,
but I shall make a fable for my womb.

Man Pointing

(after Giacometti)

Now to this city I came in the month of April.
It was complete, both crib and burial urn.
The bright lead walls, hale winds from rivers

below sheer precipices of correct glass.
Gray lions lay at the foot of fountains.
My little cat sisters offered themselves in the streets.
From cabarets young lords with horns rode out,
young lords with triplicate tongues.

Ravelins of laughter, the drunkard's face etched
on medallions of bleak Manhattan
Green rooms where I sat, circumvented by time,
as birds and shadows keep inviolate the inch
beyond desire, move without progression.

I shall study the gallery of my cells, those angry violins.
I burn a disk of incense smelling of jasmine and rose.

The Age has practiced vivisection on my brain
Who can piece it together, fished from drains, pawn shops
and storm sewers? Gods in crosses, numbers, epilepsy?
The inkblot on the brain, the astringent salvation.
Red of Cain upon coke ovens
and the windless tree of smoke,
of incubating mists, ripe thorofares.

Momently dying, fragmenting, screening earth
for assorted eggs, pebbles, ores.
Fossils in ice, rust in the magnet's core.

Combing out the fine hair of death, the reentry
after passion fails, black patinas of tongue

But now my white hand is under the cat
for the fever of her young,
in the pigeon's pelvis full of ripening yolks.

Today I dance in the street,
feeding out my hair as maypole ribbons for children,
behind me the wind shouldering
me uphill to the roman park.

Annie Hollow

I have arrived at the beginning; the guidepost is not set up;
the next town may not even be; I shall look for the stone
that marks the quarter-section and dials the sun.
The gold cloud of the east favorable to the intention
of my fathers and their women
who clamored like birds at dawn,
the men with gilded faces,
chewing the oakleaf for the mouths of bleating children,
the sky's pap fallen on the pasture of the mares,
trampled and woven into ropes of hair.

Windlasses of light haul up the sun
in buckets from the millpond's tidy races
and wheat germs flood with light the insistent stone.
To great circular burrs turning light
the women and children carried grain and rested
beside the stream that purified the stone
and rinsed the moonrings from the eyes of the mares
that all became gentle and kissed the bit
and they would set the youngest child under their feet.

I roamed through Annie Hollow kept by ruins,
finding the first day sandstone chimneys
and firedogs steeped in lye. The second day
I thought of more filial sons who married cousins,
whose children barked at squirrels while I roamed childless.
I roamed dark Annie Hollow and I sang
to witch the stone that marks the quarter-section.
There my fathers braided ropes of hair
to haul the sun, the socket's requiem
in red chalices of eyes that saw the land's broad wings
a downy heaven for those claybank mares
that rode their caskets hard.
They pelt my oakleaf with their fragrant blood!
And I sang with the red fox at dawn,
the oakleaf stamped on my forehead like the neigh of those mares
running through my mind's dust
in the very whitest day of my knowing

DEATH OF THE FARM WOMAN

Same bones, same face, same hair
I touch now, after the embalmer

lying level body, tame to the dumb frame
of the metal trestle

Railway crossings and bus intersections
where you waved sons away, old woman

Went to bright town, pinched timid dimes
To cheap cafeterias we traveled, thought them rich

But our gardens, the fruit of!
sat paring apples after sundown

said for saying, word for word
in country, Mother of dandelions

How we ran! where the water found us, with me under your heart,
young startled girl, waiting for my eyes to open

Not any clod any weed any dry furrow any spraying weed
or clod's crumble, not any stick of wood wears your hand again

So easy, to lift you now on my eyes
as the sun changes

lift you above bronze handles of your casket, above plastic grass
to a green place, on your own dumb sayso

As you stay still here, breathless
in the presence of cedar,

clay to my clay,
your meadow arms hold silence to our stillest leaves

your love-dried lips, brought up with wax, do not say
You sew these ending stitches through my lips

SLEEP IN AUGUST

Where veined rocks pulse in the sun's aftermath
the dry air moves across the earth;
leaves tick the visible days
here in time's motionless always;
among slow-burning stones in the quiet rise
of leaves, on their green frieze,
only the hooves know August's iron dances
in a flow of light over sleek bodies and wire fences
that will hang up, to bleed and clot,
in nibbling thaw and pelt-slipping rot,
crippled dogs and foxes
at the loose ends of cold chases;

in the hot yards the men's and women's hazy
faces and the honeyed children's crazy
voices swarm under a ceiling of fire;
the chained fields and nailed-down houses hear
the axe in chaste trees as they tear
and fall with a dark smear
of green against sunset, in the wasp hum
and kerosene smell of August;

sheep doze in horror of maggots in the locust
groves, and the fields mold their stones
into elemental forms,
self-contained and open and free from the incantation
of this delirious season
that runs riot in my veins, turns me to stone;

high in the trees dark birds dream
the clay of silence into presences
like tragic frogs; in the hollow sky
dead stars arrange themselves like men and animals going by
slanted in myths; then if, stopped by no watches,
I lie down on thin grain
do not wake me with promises of green.

SUNDAY

Is it five o'clock on the sun?

— Ludwig Wittgenstein

What is Out My Window

City of Churches   Sundown   October

Across the street a belfry holds warm pigeons
A tall stone house with green ivy and yellow marigolds
and a vacant lot beside a hospital,
a crabgrass short-cut for children
Two come across, one carrying his arm
over the other's shoulder,
in his left hand a softdrink bottle

Small girls in Mary's blue cross here
I cross myself, and smile

The belfry holds its signal iron
        over dented cars
In this house we are skilled workers
At night we discuss the tolerances of machines

The Way Here, and Here

Here I am schooled
Here I am paroled,
a boy led my mules,
in the distance pitchforks
and old hats, dogs barking
among wrecked automobiles

The time it took to arrive here
is the moment of seeing
morning barns and winter mud
where ewes were lambing
a dog eating a rabbit
in the rain,
trees with drooping shoulders

then Italian Renaissance houses
with cornices and pediments
scrolled in the iron evening
of streets without hoofprints

and houses of commerce
with carved names of the founders,
their hope of continuance
in photographs of daughters
in khaki riding habits,
sons in uniform, but always on leave

Here I am taught the manners
of rooms by day or week

In the university
Life Science is taught
and Human Behavior
But who will teach Death Science,
Luck and Chance?
the last light in an eye?
the afterlife of hair?

I make mirrors that keep faces
I tell hair
I collect the colors that scale from houses
I weave baskets like the veins of children and hearts
I want to be waxed and preserved
I want children like candles to illumine my breath

I have become a caller of telephones
with library ideas
There are so many houses!
with scheduled birds and sorrows
The frozen streets keep no footprints
How far from nothing to something?
From ice to sun again

The speed of dark is the same as the slow of light
cast on the statue of Lincoln

before the public library
near the used-car lot
by the skating arena
near insistent music

At five in the morning across the grave river
icy grass binds the ankles of mules
and the tombs of new people
and ricks of gray straw stand by the zero barns
Snow falls on the river, a moment white, then goes

My Union Card

Laborer, cousin, kinsman,
this is for you:

journeyman carpenter, I leave you my hammer
      to nail pictures of nude whores
      on the walls of motels

house painter, cousin three years dead, I lay
      the brushes you gave me on your unmarked grave

posthole digger, take these gloves

truck driver, take my pills, whiskey and weary roadhouses

physicist, father, here are your tri-focal glasses
      behind which the light waves sound

gardener, mother, here are your bonnet and hoe
      for dandelion and plantain

pie baker, with your flower's name
      dead among your redbirds and spices,

we are wood by working wood
we are stone by lifting stone
we are air by breathing
we are simple and free as love
we are lonely and crippled as love

we are strong as love
we are orphaned to love

Some of us are dead now, some living among losses
May our love not be lost among my last voices

An Arrival

Through wired gladioli I hear music
I see my uncle's face in his casket
He had planted an early garden
His granddaughter sang for his funeral,
        her young voice drowned by the train
        that ran west towards St. Louis

That music was serious
        from the lips of a schoolgirl
        with fried onion rings on her breath

I can imagine music
What I can't imagine
is what I shall have to write
today for my uncle

A noun is the name of a person, place or thing
This is untrue
I know many untrue things
Therefore, by farmers in a baconed kitchen, I was chosen
        to write the obituary:

under a blue neon light my uncle lies
among mud-caked pigs, grain bins,
gladioli and dung, and a cowbell
wandering in the unincorporated town

The speed of the train to St. Louis
burns ragweeds between the crossties
Nobody can travel west from here unless a flagman
stands half a mile uptrack, waving

I wave there
Grammar?
Music?
I cannot hear

I Imitate Life

I walk down oak stairs in old houses
I walk up child-strewn streets
I wear a coat when the wind is cold
I recall how to smile in the houses of friends
I write many letters that I do not mail
I play cards, drink, throw black money
        on green tables as I lose
Loss is my skill

Let every man be perfect at something

Telegram

I have seen sidewalk mirrors condense my life like truth
Raining   Gray here
Rain   Gray   Night   Love   Stop
But love cannot stop
Trust you are well   Leaves colorful here this fall
The metal mirrors   I have sat in the automatic booth
and had my picture taken: four exposures for a quarter
hoping I might get a good one to send   Sorry they did
        not turn out   Will try again in near future   Love

The hair of the trees falls on my shoulders
Little rains fall on my shoulders
Eyes, too

Have not heard   Have not seen   Nothing to report
except the mirrors   Tried the photo machine again
today   Eyes not on the red arrows in the mirror
All wrong   Will try again soon   Love

Sometimes I wonder if you know
how the mirrors look at street-level

How can I tell you?
What holds honesty away?

I smell wet dogs
I smell alcohol
I smell the beautiful scent of your brain

The pictures came, wet and dim, out of the machine
Will not try again
I have been

An Absence

Knowledge fails   Touch fails   Vision fails   Love fails

Knowledge is no book against loss
Touch is no hand against loss
Vision is no eye against loss
Love is no sacrament against loss

I close my books   I fold my hands   I close my eyes
    I fold my loves

Valentine

Too many kinsmen asked me to say our sorrows

Those who sat in shawls near coal stoves under small American
    flags and photographs of sons at war
Those who filled glass dishes with rock candy
    for no mouths
Those who listened in varnished parlors to piano music
Those who played electric guitars
Those who shot themselves in the feet in Italy
Those who said I love you without meaning I or love or you
Those who lay with ears full of blood and sun in Africa,
    unspent postage in their fatigues

and my cousin, whose submarine delivered him to tearing fish

What Do I Know?

What is my knowledge? Parents I can't find?
Brothers I visit once a year?   A sister who
is a Pauline Christian?   A wife anointed by pain?
And a child who was taken away?

What shall I say
of the many beautiful
I name equal and beautiful?
They are changing
They are always changing
What is my knowledge?
To say my love, with awe

I Greet Myself Near the Beginning

I know nothing but love, a thing
        of grass and brain and hands, open

I know nothing but love, a thing
        of schoolrooms and chalk and reading

I know nothing but love, a gallery
        of photographs of dead children

I know nothing but love, a wallet
        that identifies me past recalling

I Greet You, City

I did not ask if I could be
Many times I have regretted that I became
But there is no escape from knowing   And
I knew always in this place I would happen

I am your house painter and cement finisher
I have worked here these ways
I tell your time on the dials of my eyes
I have bled dark residence, City

My shadow crosses your spires at noon
My shadow crosses your taverns at midnight
Your streets breathe me in

Sister, Pray for Me

Sister, your white headband, your black dress, your unread lips,
    your steel-rimmed glasses,
your short pointless journeys into my colorful and dying world,
    your cold beads, your delicate chains!
Not that we have stopped on the street where I pass you
    each day, or spoken

We know many things that are not spoken

O, stranger in Christ, what have you given up?
What have I embraced?

Sister, in your dear Christ's only name, pray forgiveness
    for your tolerable chains and my intolerable freedom!

Adoration

My life is a cathedral
My life bends in chronic adoration
My life is stained green by copper flashing
My life is supported by flying limestones
My life crosses itself, and stares

Beautiful child, while pigeons murmur, tell me
the woman ways of your quick radiance!

Mondays we begin all over

The street is littered with music programs
    where they have fallen

I lead with hands   Who follows?
I cannot look back   Who might be where?

Army stores wrap me in wool

Across the street pigeons nestle
    under a churchbell

If I sit in a deaf room with blind walls this Sunday,
awed by the slow morning radiance,
who can say no, if I say yes?

CEREMONIES (II)

A REVEL

Black trees ice-barked and flaming shake braids of hair
thick with evening odors of soft coal over my bemused house,
hush down the white walls and nut floors and pepper-ripe sills,

hold my cistern-sized and perishable earth still until rabbits
        scream above and moles run under orchards of snow
and my chronic harvest stores little false deaths, the fertile
        comedies of all saviors' third mornings
when under ice tomb-wrecking seeds wake and storm sunwards
        their green legends,
hold clear stars in purlieus of adventure, glitter in the fern-kept
        history of my trees and as peacefully burn and die,
where rabbit scuts burst white in the black hickories
and the gamecocks' shanks grow electric in snow, thin-stamened,
the pale round signatures of combs and hackles new sunflowers'
        gazes turn;

        here in a funnel of leaves the white roof water carves
brittle wreaths incensed at the candors of dawn
in early resonances ascending of gold green shanks budding
        with spurs;

immersion of morning here gives back sense to my swift creatures
that as quickly die as corn tassels and blood-burst rabbits
        curled in sleet;

        O empty birds, cry in the matted heads of my trees;
acclaim my deaf gullies with your little tongues! charm
at dawn the quickening woman in my house riotous with eggyolks;
rake your harsh thighs; be always keen for cutting;
fly in the perfection of your injuries;
while my landed hand throws pale grain upon snow,

preen the bleak land you tow your exulting tongues over;
walk lightly on nests that lie in blushes of straw, full;

the woman in my house is beautiful
because she can turn herself into a tree or a mother or a slut;
I think of the grave delight of being mirrored in her eyes
    deep as honey jars,
haughty and sorrowful because she knows she will as soon die
    and her borrowed ribs sieve minerals quietly;

here between ever reweaving root latitudes, anther and filament
prize her wholly mortal and heavily scented and young,
going by sun and season,
to whom my drunken ponds wave breathless violences.

AND IF I
SEE HER

SMALL RAIN

Child, under grass, always at night
your close cries and falls of clear hair
lock me with love; my bare fields rove;
my locked love under grass cries
and falls always in your deep hair at night;
my roving fields lock you here round my love
in the burst green of trees where my nailed eyes hold
their crosses up in a stray rain to catch your water face
here in our broken knowing, in my ransom hours
      of rain standing
always at the green falls of night grass
above my near love, roving towards the broken horizon
in its rainy hearse that carries me lost in the fall
      of bare horizons
round our green sad morning marriage, beautiful child!

May the brown faces of broken clay
that hold anxious flowers on sudden clear graves
above rusted wire frames and green twisted ribbons,
left helter-skelter beside the brave hearse,
reflect your greenest hopes against this cold new time
      of slow leaves curling
and the haphazard faces of flowers that mock
the careful movements of your unlucky thumbs.

O broken child, cut free of our eyeless children, O love!
suffer your beauty; suffer the greed of green to kill
      at the ends of your weeping hands.

DEATH IN OREGON

Girl Riding

The young trees are dry and light,
In the growing season no rain makes this land run green
Summer holds the gray odor of dying grass

The wind tacks dead twigs to fences
The branch of the willow tree is light
I lift it above the dark girl's head
She is light and dry
I am not burdened by her body riding my shoulders
Often her long hair falls in my eyes
Her black hair drowns the thin grass of this barren country
Light trees rise on my hands and let her go by
I hold a willow branch out of her eyes
Her eyes hold oceans that tilt her body riding my shoulders,
When she is angry her legs whip my ribs like the thin brown kelp
      I cracked on the beach
I remember the blacksnake whips of my boyhood when cruelty
      was the first lash of kindness
The girl riding my shoulders under the willows has a god
She prays her god to bless me
She weeps often at night
She is weightless, a benediction of sunlight on my body
The pale leaves of willow I lift let her dark head pass
Her ocean eyes tilt down to the unstable earth
Fish keep the curve of her lips
Her head looks down to this sparse earth
She weeps at night
She asks her god to bless me
All is perilous
Her god might not answer
She might not love me tomorrow
She may not remember the difference between loving a god
      and a man
Silently our skillful heads are helped to go by the lightness
      of the young trees in my hands
I hold up branches out of her eyes
I feel into my ribs a small leaning woman whose face follows
      the earth at my feet
She asks her god to bless my journey
Her hair harbors me
I have carried her a long way
I have drunk light, eaten air, to carry her
How to make clear the soul I do not have—
      past or present, now or to be created—

is the walking I condemn myself to
The freedom to walk the past away by measuring nothing
        is the journey
I have carried her across America to this Western death
She lives in peril
I am careful
I hold trees away from her small face
She looks down to the dry earth at my next step
She knows she is safe where she is
She asks her god to bless me
I think her lips can wake up earthworms, turtles and carp
She puts small hands on my face
Her hair reaches down to my heart
She leans into the place where I took out my last rib
I hear her innocent confessions
I am a strange priest
My habit is her hair drawn over me
My altar is her elbow
The host I lift is a willow

Portrait

A poor man's daughter with rich hair,
proud eyes and movements of her dark body,
able to hold a man, children and books in her arms,
and open her face to children,
and place her wrist, a ribbon to mark books,
and stare up through the shadow of my face
with the curiosity of a young vine to see the sun—

I listen to the leaves her voice grows

Among formal aisles of roses my rising and cutting hand,
holding color, waved you warm
I carved your face and polished it with my hands
I died in all the little bones inside you
I saw color return your morning eyes
You sang small
How many words do your fingers count round?
Where does your god go when it rains?
How do you grow real roses in your mouth?

Long flowers with your little tongues,
Where do you go now in hunger?
Once the winey heads arranged themselves,
They did not imitate any created thing

Not by Bread

Where I live the earth is flat and does not move round any sun
There is no time My father and mother have become my own
children As I am now your son and offer you my eyes

How did you find my time being in the earth, its lover,
and go there before me for my last being to find over
and over among fallen trees and stranded birdcries?

Leaves soon will look down from saplings this new spring
Your fingerprints on my eyes will not let them green me
In this city I will miss the clear sound of bees

Unlanded now, among grumbling rats and dirty birds
In a city at this brazen distance from trees
I taste toothpicks and copper spit At night stray dogs rise

and laugh round the horizon of my first country
Birds rattle their stony wings, and dwindle
Down the cold neon avenue, the surprise

of a red light crosses in and out my window
from a police car, stopped in the street below,
red for the heart that dies

on the stretcher the policemen carry blackly through a crowd
The murdered man repeats his triumphal ride
through an aisle of leaning faces and the siren's blaze

My Christian, my love, my mother-child of blue,
where is our worship? between the slow
hush of our mouths? between faces without lies?

Take from my hands you always believe this green dress
and a wild bird to roost your wooden crucifix,
huntress and Christian in your new green guise

Light woman, last heart I carry, beautiful and dark, take
if your god lives, lives, O for your god's last red sake
take and breathe love, love, O grow fast our lost and taken lives!

A RITUAL

The Dead Stars

The language of harvest was sugar, having
   no intervals, no melodies,
perfect for insects and the steady airs
   they carve;
they forget to sting, to breed;
the ardent air is time made visible
among the white branches of apple trees;

being natural, you understood that world's
   terrors
and invented intervals of song to avoid
   the drone of too-small wings,
but you could not escape selection and death;

August was a mirage of black starlings
that roosted thin irises of glass,
the stuffed owl's eyes above the lintel,
scaled feet rooted in the watery light,
   a twilight of buckled wings;
you thought of distasteful grubs in tree bark
   and of barbaric invasions;
you saw a bird drop, bounce on the mast,
   roll a dry inch;
lice abandoned its body and began the long climb
up the tree where blood is unfaded and sweet;

below, still quills beckon a putrid breeze;
while you watched. thinking: Cherries!
earth sieved thin reddest water
        from a drying beak
and, among apple cores, little pigs found
        your fabled star.

The Meadow

My girl lay in the sun;
that burden was too loud;
she took pennies from her knotted kerchief
and laid them on her eyes

though she was not dead
or thought of herself perishing
until she left the sun and was cool
        and could forget
the hot astonishment of the coins;

a tigerish bee dandled from the stem
        of a white clover,
white silence mounted by an orange sound,
water drinking an ingot of the sun;

a cloud swam past the sun's cornice;
a tree spilled petals down the inverted sky;
a tailtwisting wind mouthed the petals,
cream for my girl, sprouting breasts, to drink,
for my young girl to rub on her knowing face,
my child to curd with praise her wishbone's meat.

The Scolding

Archangel of summerside,
the woman threw a beaded shawl on her head and came
waving a finger, preaching to the ground,
a farmer's wife, unafraid of sailors
who fed black cats the heads of pearly fish;

blue tattoos on the red-brown arms
gave her wrath grace
against the feeding of shipboard cats and raccoons;

my girl, high in the twigs of the mast, silent,
pictured the dustless parlor, the piano,
the pared fruit wax-like in glass jars in the cellar,
blue milk in crocks on the porch, the wooden horse
she rode by lamplight to keep warm;
then the stench of hot bananas, tarantulas
    drowned in leaves,
the water verminous and scrawled with oil
moved those dominions of her skirt
towards darkness where the rib of summer caves,
sails bursting; the surly waterspouts
in their plummet grow long sighs of wrath's
    grim zodiac;

my young girl's pennants mourn
bailing cans full of sailors poured at her feet,
the carcass of the world sprinkled with lime
against swellings and the yawn of ribald cats;
drifted in powder and lilac water,
my girl looks from the dark tent of age-sweetened flesh
    like sick girls' dreams.

The Corpse

Your branchy bones had not yet hardened,
    your sea-gills dried;
you cannot suck and spit and screw your head
    like an owl;
you cannot walk;
you cannot pick up scissors with your hands
    to cut out cardboard sailors;
you cannot speak;

your head may as well have been a blue balloon
    with eyes, nose, mouth painted on;
it floated away, light with mystery;

but these are only signs of a headstone's rout;
I take for dimples time's smite on stone.

The Hill

You lie under the hill
and love conceals you fearfully;
you who wore my ring
lie under the hill
and love, a deaf musician,
stares at your beadless silence;
you lie under the hill
and love disdains a hovering
of starlings on telegraph wires
at their punctual distances;
your straight hair undertaken,
you lie under the hill
and love stops ticking;

for you the ticking stopped
like melting icicles;
for you the humming cold wires
do not signal
across your lucid winter;

for the poverty of your dear love,
for whom love is dazzled by—
silence, radiance, doldrum of candle
light on window-hosted snow are all.

LETTER FROM THE LOVED WOMAN OF AVENUE A

Please defrost the refrigerator
Please water the plants with tepid water
The violets should be watered from the bottom lips
    of their dishes up
Eat the bacon and eggs   I even bought you grits
    second shelf
Get much work done

I love you and will see you at the AMTRAK

The sick nightmare jive you suffered through with me
        our first year when I was a "talky" girl!
Oh, but I feel so grown up now and send to you
        all my collective loves

I spent you blind, Baby, $2.35 for a catfish dinner
        in a little hole in the wall in South Carolina
In between alka seltzers I looked—like you told me—
        at the sluggish brown rivers and green pines
        and watched my reflection in the motel windows
        all very tricky because so crowded with despair

Along the railway from Richmond to Danville
        there's a stretch—is that the word?—
        of land, well wooded and hilly
        for you to look into and possibly buy
        to build our house on
        corn and beans for you, an herb garden for me
        and I promise not to burn the house down
        like your apartment on Sullivan Street that night

Please remember the train is due at 6:50 p.m.
Please know that I understand another kind of fire
        in my belly, the red coal of our child

TO A YOUNG WOMAN OF TWENTY
I CARRIED ON MY SHOULDERS AT FIVE

I was glad to see you
despite your Cowboy boots
Western jacket and hat
and your air of being interested
in nothing at all

Less glad to see your companions,
spineless young pups, trailing,
sniffing as if you were in heat,
not bold enough to mount you

I wish you more than young men
who think a well-spent night
is burning napkins in ashtrays,
who giggle, tote sleeping bags
not in Wyoming but Brooklyn
and cultivate holes in their socks

It's probably lucky for both of us
That I had no chance to speak
with you privately because
I might have said, "Timothy Leary
loves Doris Day" and you would
have had to run me through
with your Army Surplus bayonet

ODE TO THE TEENIES OF TOMPKINS SQUARE

Hissing agony to psychiatrists
girls without earth for their feet
women, ungreen, with hard knees
posters of Spain on their walls
hands unopened to live flowers
compulsively closed on men's cocks—
they pump out the male stream briefly
and lie down, sad and unwanted
grit in their angry eyes
fixed on their own crucifixions
no prayers in their dirty shawls

Girls in their New York uniforms
male from the crotch down
in their Lees and Levis
manly buckles and high boots
female from the navel up
long hair, Peruvian blouses

Girls eating 40¢ pizza
their vinegar-stung cunts
dreaming of penetration
the gaumed girls of dough and cheese
hopeful wistful and snarling
blowing their brains out in brick cells
to the whisper of roaches
and the odor of marijuana

Russian and Roman fathers
teach reverence for the liferoot
how to fondle caress and jack it
suck power and swallow the magic
Some like to go down for kicks
their vaginas and colons so shot full
that only their mouths remain hungry

Nailed to the cold green benches
hurt-hearted girls spitting semen
huddled in the radiance
of psycho secret loneliness
their chorused clitori ringing
like tiny altar bells

THE FIRST DAY OF CHRISTMAS

One turtle dove
two turtle doves
three turtle doves
in the hawks' talons
Come to NYU
Come to NYU
Be raped on Park Avenue
You girls of Forest Hills
come to NYU
Be raped in Washington Mews
Lie in your apartments

blood caked on your mouths
You girls of Virginia
come to NYU
Be raped in the Port Authority
your first night in the city
present your injury
in red hieroglyphics
to St. Vincent's emergency
Come to NYU
You girls from Vermont
come to NYU
Be raped in MacDougal Alley
Come get your comeupppance
Come to NYU
You girls of New Jersey
Come to NYU
Be raped in Sheridan Square

    Flail your Head
    left to right
    grit your teeth
    bite your tongue
    below a scream
    held in the talons
    of a diving hawk
    and beaten blue
    Come to NYU

Any girl too dumb
to want to have some fun
deserves to be slapped
with the butt of a gun
Come to NYU
You girls from Carolina
come to NYU
be raped on Bleecker Street
get gonorrhea free
from the hawk's tail
Leave a blood trail
on a white towel

Thrash your head
to and fro
Come to NYU
The rapist is brief
furious he tears in
lays knife upon pillow
where you can see
He knocks out your teeth
Nothing you can do
Come to NYU
Loeb Student Center
NYU
One Jewish girl
One Jewish Girl
epitome of beauty
One Jewish girl
raped in Patchen Place
on the cobblestones
her body bruised and cut
concealed by makeup
Eyes on the floor
of Loeb Student Center
pills in her purse
ready to OD
feeling filthy all over
Gonna OD
Can't phone your parents
to tell them where you are
Who is so reckless as
to walk in Washington Square?
Can't tell her father
Can't tell her mother
Can't tell her fiancé
Gonna OD
One turtle dove
one cyanide
one cyanide
One turtle dove
screams in the talons
of a hungry hawk

One cyanide
pill will do
Bye little girl
Bye little girl
After you OD
I shall stand on First Avenue
to see your hearse go by
out to Long Island
where you still shall lie
Bye, little Jew
I love you
One turtle dove
One singing wing
of one turtle dove
caught by a hawk
Feathers and blood

One turtle dove
One foreign trip
one trip to Europe
try to forget
but cannot forget
one painful cry
one bloody thigh
Endless foreign trip
sent by parents
to Switzerland
the remainder of your life
One turtle dove
one degradation
In Switzerland
you will remain
You can never regain
self or the knife
laid on your pillow
Invaded and thrown
you cannot return
Orthodontist can
replace your teeth
cracked on St. Mark's Place

but you cannot forget
and you cannot return
to the lazy swell
of a lordly day

Come to Fun City
Come to NYU
Get an audition
on how to break your spine
Come to NYU
Here in Bellevue
I can't see the sky
I live only because you
come to visit me
Ward NO-5 is lonely
The shrinks feed me pills
to sedate me
no psychiatric help
just the powerful downers
to wipe out Connecticut
where as a kid
I winked at fireflies
All night the crazies wail
I keep going only
because you visit me
One turtle dove
mad as Ophelia
singing her water songs
One turtle dove
caged for life
in Bellevue Nut Ward
NO-5
I tuck you under my wing
For you I sing
Silent white
Doric columns
Doric white
silent columns
Fluted stone Doric stands
Stately Bellevue

lost hospital
of NYU
One way in
No way out
of NO-5
Bellevue Nut Ward
silent and white

On the first day of Christmas
my sweet pets gave to me
All my pretty ones
gave to me
One turtle dove

MARRIAGE SONG

The Hunter, the Catch

We go from swelter to freeze
My woman strikes to fix green
    fires that cringe
Our son holds a hatchet that cuts
    blood, if I let
Cold mornings I kiss his belly
I kiss his mother's eyes

Raw, after that:
Run upon drunk hill boys
    who promise to kill me
    if they catch me out again
I show my woman how
    to fire the .410
Her Indian eyes don't blink
    at the full-choke lightning

No deer today
Sundown blinds snow
Fire in my house

Oak smoke climbs to the North Star
I lean to the window's hard light
    where two loves wait me
    with hands the same size

I track down the woman's tongue
My neck wears her gold medallion
    stamped with a fertile stork
She presents her son as a gift
I load him on my neck
Her delight is we run and kiss
She wants me to find her
    hidden in rowdy black hair
She lifts me on fine-honed legs
Her teeth grin like rain

I'm earth-spawn
I belong to pine

My body their rainbow,
wife & son will cry
my knocked box down

Marriage Song

To the light white spring bloom falling over the dumb
pages of winter-turned books and simple signs of hands
consecrated by a man and woman walking under spring rain,
    cousins to minnows and wet calves

their pulpits formed in religious rocks
and surrounded by cattle, wet noses down—
the color of hair, the smell of melting snow
and to rusted mouths, soon as winter wears out mud
into unfolding apples and cicadas, sunlight on sudden tongue!
the blindness of, the strength of spliced arms
carries grain and salt to young muzzles,
lets go the regaling fire of tufts, sprouts, perilous buds,
going free the green awful shine

If I try tobacco & corn harvest with sore arms
    from a house where a woman & boy stray & steam
Take in love for berry eyes & mahogany legs,
    candy canes, wear & tear of child bones

I'm coaxed into a year of grains' yearn
    & sullen humility under the sun
Gloved in wife & child blowing lung-frost
I cut green hickory to sing
    on the hearth

Promised infinite lucky Spring
I tune my carcass
My young son crows
My wife swings & shines
I dive down my heart's run
    & drown in their sweet spit

Pavane for a Dead Princess

> *... too soon*
> *After so short time of breath*
> *To house with darkness and with death.*
>   — John Milton

How slowly is carried the leveled girl
    in a black plastic sack
My lost wife killed, barely down under Kentucky,
    cadaver at rest
    while little mares dance near green Paris

Now if the barest mercy imagined by priests of Orpheus
    centers on the yet unrisen body, the silt of drowning
    still on his tongue,
you shall not lie untended as water & stones roll
    timeless awash at the far cliffs of Earth

You were the ghost of the rank garden
The tongues of my grasses spoke to you

Of all the flowers you chose marigolds
I dreamed of sickles & weeds cowered for your sake
A red sun swam in New River
In the reeds redwing blackbirds called to Marvell:
    "Carpe diem, carpe diem"
This photo of you was shot in Mt. Jefferson's
    wild rhododendron
Animals smiled when you fed
We were close as lice

I'd be a long way from my poor
a long time lost from my poor
too long away from the dire hurts & miseries
The silent night-lawn, the timid flowers,
    the muted thrushes
Too far away from the burnished skin of the girl
    whose cheer shames Eve in her garden
I cannot go from these neighbors & pities for whom I swing
    the thurible of love

All things past are unreal as a flown bird that leaves
    nothing behind, like the footprints of a star
I have fed the mouth that bites me
I have no history & the stains I seem to leave behind
    are illusion

I am throat-deep in decay:
New Yorkers who took The Beatles seriously
A friend who still listens to Mozart
A Jew who listens to Gregorian chants on Sundays
A friend who blows a flute but never listens to Coltrane
Titless women lean toward the same
Where do they think this world is?

Find it off
O, find it off!
Water pure, flow it off
Counting rural mailboxes
The ritual burning of old stalks
Stone leaves have fallen from corinthians
    at the fathering ledges of the world

A hungry hearse glides
A white tombstone abates
Cedar dove, sigh her still, still arms
Risus sardonicus mocks the happy smile of fallen Eve

Nothing is given that is not taken back
Therefore, fools of this life, look at my face, if you dare

Free of all things save this breath, I sing for you,
    Ella Maria Mercado,
upon the vault of your spirit's atrium
the fire that is never quenched
& the worm that cannot die

GREEN GIRL

> *to Antonia Squitieri (1951–1971)*
>
> *Passing. One. We are passing. Two. From sleep we are
> passing. Three. Into the wideawades warld from sleep we
> are passing. Four. Come, hours, be ours!*
>
> *But still. Ah diar, ah diar! And stay.*
>
> — James Joyce, from *Finnegan's Wake*

Come, Little Leaves

Hill high as the sun colors day
swarms of cold gold leaves blind me
    and sweet oak smoke
The stems of meadows' torn weeds fume

What will down will down
    from the seed crown

Beside me a green girl says, Don't cut it,
    that weed wants itself

Her eyes know happy happy! I'll not kill

For her sake I take off my gloves in any cold
Her body is the only ruler
        I imagined as a boy I could measure things by
Her ears are my music
Her tongue is my spit & speech
Her ankles tie my bouquet

Beauty isn't said
Beauty is tried like lard from the carcass of a pig

I see them, all my things riching and rotting
how I know them today & will become
Now in reveled October their colors are drawn

But to see her my her, her gladness to touch
        in a wild field
is to be myself warmest all at once
and tuck her smiling knees in my hands
And she is all bunched up and happier than a squirrel
        with alerter eyes
Little leaves parachute to her hands

Under the Meadow

In the frost night clear as the scent of cloves
little heads cry ice and curl down like my cold own
They have more petals to confess yes to
They are more beautiful than I, even in my own rooted say-so
Yet I, too, nod my head to my own brown season
        and lie down in a drift of thin waned leaves
I crumble, too

While the green girl takes my frown away
and brings back all the slaked rages I wore out to scar
and I see a little sight and I fix the star of myself
for her wherever she has in wonder gone

I'm here to find her visiting punk and roots and late shoots
        by the water

My forehead crosses her into light's late comedown
Come full dark shine, we'll learn how to crawl
    where the peaches buried their coals' magics

Magic—I have a claim on some, some

All things alive are the same tame
Death is the broken eye and the brain's small rain

My loveling goes ways by this falling stream
O, shudder, grass shelter!
Wind, make room
Hush, bush
Don't catch her breath
Don't take the blame
Wave my sweet heart on

Ode to Autumn

Fire of sumac, and the green running
Still days shine like copper
The bright white night grass leans
    over gravestones like lain down lambs

The dog I dragged dead away
    has caved in to fangs and bone——
    no buzzards, no rain
    Pure sun carved him

Into this leaf gulf the burnt and burning stars
call fire and tall weeds burn their crowns
like girls under kisses and hands

Girl, give me samples
My bed smells like apples

Here in a turmoil of sweet willing swill
mad bees suck mud
Pear-fisted children grin and run
at their blossom ends

A cold wind blows in
Soon my grapes will tease foxes

The cricket and I are alive because we make noises
I pretend Indiana didn't cripple my poor head
1 walk under a moth's quick kiss
        and bats cheer me with a loud clapping
        this cold evening

Late light rings the axe of my father
Dark settles the gentle flowers of my mother
And what light for my own Hell-coming?
Sedges, I drew your short straw
My inferiority makes me cry
down a tin gully of yellow school buses,
a boy who hoped for little more
than a clear idea of his cold Harm-coming
And what for my singing?
The hungry birds look down, and are fed

I've not been false since yesterday
I tell a lie only once a day
        and that to myself
The leaves shudder at my truthfulness
Marigolds greet me and bring their friends
We talk yellow

I'm not going anyplace
except to throw lime on my lost dog
I'm swayed like a wheathead to loving and wishing
        for light
Rotting hide tears me
Peeled fangs, onions, hay I throw
I bend under little broken bushes

The owl is full of shrill spittle
The crayfish bubble slime
Stars whine a far far light
I throw bottles from a fast car
I call and catch fire

My sorrow plays, Here comes,
       ready to die, or not!

Now in brutal October
Keats, Wolfe, Thomas, move over
I'll drive this time
Detroit Iron, don't stall
While white maggots swim
through the pine gloom
haul my loveling home

And If I See Her

And if I see her in any picturing of blue eyelid
hanged lip or any felt slippery go to hip or ribsense
brown breasts or any smelled go to thick swollen hair
or gummy blue eyelids or her rain-sodden heart, felt
little sudden pump of now and then and then again, sucking gore
and full felt woman nosing my neck or she lay at night
afraid unless nose bled breath on me or she shaded my country
ear and gander neck in a morass of rotten cotton breath
running alive with love's worms
And if I hear her in better frost air walking by my side
or at midnight's crow and ecstasy where her low voice came
I stammer you, my love, you with my love's surprises, yes
and guess how much I stammer you into my only haved haven,
my love, and one white cat I wish on you to nap at your feet I wish
you for a funny trick or why cat and I roll over for you with your
       promise
of food even though our god fell down the sun in a tree out the window
and after your bent tracks lost sight night after goodnight
And when I taste the hare-like sweat of her body spined down
and olive forehead and the salt of her tears and turned aside
to the carcass of a dog deepening under high wheels of buzzards
over my meadow and yes then into my mouth the thin liquid of her
terrible tongue
For there was a swarm of bees in the belly of the dead dog
And smell her tears, the girl's weeping, kiss her trouble,
dearest daughter of my shot heart, bad head, my last living loving
and all ferment of our short goings and comings

And if l feel her body uprooted in my arms,
my hands lift, my lungs breathe into her drowning and save

Eyeless in Indiana

I saw them fall full, the tree over the leaf,
 the well over the water, the girl over the cloth
I let my head fall back full in joy
My bones genuflected to her spine
I gave her an apple smile for her cider,
 for her joined and jointed body
 like a petal puzzle
 all yellow as tobacco

See my marbles, my slingshot, my bike
See an old radio that ladled the syrup
of the Hit Parade into frosty spireas
 beyond the yard fence
See my Indiana
Central Dream of this continent
It's called "Stardust"

The Harley big bike rides dead Dean
The Big O dribbles a ball at Crispus Attucks
Here are the slaughterhouses of Armour and Swift
Petillo, 1935—Andretti, 1969

Let them rev, let them speed to the circus
smell of blood, castor oil in carburetors
to sullen thwarts that die men down in bottles
and the slow rot of exhausted joys

These men crawl like maggots on my once-beautiful eyes

Here are my hands
Where are the pillars?

Night Bloom

Horses tear grass near my door
Stars are so mute where they are

Stiller yet in this rotting rail forest
    my father's black tongue whistles
    his birds down at night stir

What leaves grin there!

My heart brambles the mud of my lonely body
    where only creek buds blame and care

After the high-maned corn-crazed heads go rough and cold
    of milky colts sucking while walking
    and fragile hocks dance
I go back into holy laurel
I weep at the sight of a girl's shoes in my pine house
I hear her say senseless sounds in the pitch of her love

I obey bloom in a bad head
I have made more mistakes than God

Signature

A lost dog sings and marches at night all night
    over my sinking head, my dark sunflower
He walks my cold night out. He cries and weeps
    in the stumps of dead trees
He sounds my name in the stillness of my hiding
And startled out of meat-dreams strays among hungry thorns
He sings in the absence of human voices
    and walks his nails across me whether wither these leaves
    and flooded wails to the dark hollows of my hooded hills

My head is what rides under the trees
My arm is what strikes the soil with love
My legs ask dew my next step
My mouth curls a voice to this shape
My name hides now and is hidden

O lift my head back gently and lay it down

DEAD MAN'S JACKET

Sun & shine & an otter in the lake
water where we walked & talked
Love, under sweating papayas & you were happy
    to save money
when you bought the jacket in your usual ravel
    of words
& boattail grackles in alarmed palm tassels
    swarmed up in a wink of time

Beside the hospital, clothing at the Thrift Shop
    is for sale
Girl, did you think as you fitted it over my shoulders
this 75¢ jacket came off the body of an Englishman
    who moulders here in Florida sand
    his death plundered by your happy breath?

Dear, Dear, thank you
& I shall wear this blue blazer with brass buttons
Only, I'll tear out the swell London label

VIRGIN, A BLUES

She was married in a tapestry
and her Son descended and ascended
through the woolen trees

why is She weeping?
She feels her Son's body
in the basket of her body
descend and leave her empty
of no use further to the Father
Son and Holy Spirit
She is weeping
at His ascending and descending and ascending

see in the green forest
the feathery wrist on Her head
She in her sweetness
incomparable sweetness
O wood sorrel by the white wool river
chord her sugared bones!

first for the Fathering and Fathered God
second for the Son of the feathered God
third for the Ghost with the Feathery wrist
fourth for the Earth mother of men
Wife of the First Blessed of men
O thou Hand, thou Hand of fire
touch the Quaternity who sustain us
that we may drink the wine
and eat the hot-mouthed wheat
ground in the hollow bowl smoothed by her tears.

GREENTREE'S NIGHT WATCHER

(June, softly as in)

To my wrists chain fast your criminal pulses
my dark night watcher
lock your hair, elegantly bright,
to my hands
your brown skin flay and anoint in the arbor
of my ribs caved for you each creation of the earth
and light that greens your turning body
stake your darkness to the close compass of my knowing

here all is meaningless night, meaningless day
do not hurry, night watcher
the light that gives you glory
will take it all away.

AN APPLE FOR JAN

Bright, O what quick eyes & voice
just the tip of talent, augur of the genuine
poet troubled by ice in the vein
Nervous as a snake she could make
songs on guitar yet so sad wander
hands weeping on strings into nightmare
Her night screams were silent
Only in day she taxed me for psychic rent

Block? No. A lovely American orphan
running where & when
drugs by the bale
abortion for birth control
Squirrely girl of Youth Culture
her totems: cock, rock & cocaine

Sunset on the Blue Ridge where
I hear her voice My lost winced dear
how surely I care! I go to winter
weed crowns & harvest her absence
I bite an apple, sample it like her lip

When our bodies obeyed, how fine!

Iridescent entrails of cottontails
shine on a highway
as she tears my arms & guns
a little car away
Can I weep for more loss?

I could die of felonies not committed or why
I can say it was happy seed of mutant green before I
grew sorrow-cancer

By the fire she played guitar
for the neighbors & children
Then the ache of urgency

Though you have to go
Girl, sing for me

WOMAN WITH GUITAR

for Jan

Brown are the grasses of August
The animals fall & drowse
Sweet is the scent of dried blood

Fish leap into rock castles
Cast down your eyes like pebbles
deep in the pool of your body
where the next plucked string can ripple

Over your autumn guitar
you curve a waning moon
after the sun dives down
in raspberries & wine

Weave these notes on your fingers
like a girl's cats-cradles:

Sing one for the flowers of midnight
that nobody ever sees
Sing one for the touching of tongues
Sing one for the fret of your spirit

Go to the power, lost lover,
Sing father & mother in absence
your girlhood sunk in a ritual
of bells in Pennsylvania

Strum a boychild lost & furious
Chord the stench & ache of Washington
& the fever of loneliness

Time is the measure of mercy
Small is the acre of death

CEREMONIES (III)

BLACK LEATHER

in memoriam, James Dean

In the merciless sky of his warbled days and nights
clouds imitate dreams the way light poles totem
electric deaths in the sparkling neon of jukes
over mail-order orphans in their crazy runs through
the wire wheels of motorcycles and the black leather
of shielded rampage, skyrocketed, pledged
by his last ride from California to Indiana
with his untrue Italian girl's yellow scarf tied
to his crash-helmet, going to a dirt track's scrambled race
at a little fair, for a small prize, the cloth screaming
behind him from Pasadena to his new gasoline death
ignited in paper cups among roadside weeds and in lean dust
along the monotonous shoulders of a grim highway of corn
spears, his brain suddenly still with this wild love

AMERICAN ELEGIES

WASHINGTON, 1958

Arlington Cemetery

So it may be clear and inconceivable
as murders augured in childhood's long evils
and be seen burning down cities over popcorn
        and police whistles

let it appear heavy at the bottom, stable
as women leaning to Lincoln's or Lenin's face,
wishing their sons not alive to create again
        Shiloh or Budapest,
only their own radiant intrusion among rifles

and blue as poultry hung in shop windows
imitating abundance, clear but inconceivable,
as meat cannot appear in the public imagination
        clucking or grazing
but only takes shape in the controlled light
        of ovens

as the women cannot imagine pain until it
        suddenly is

then blinding in a thicket of elbows and knees
        seeming to grow, though broken,
let it be detailed as fingerprints, firingpins
and the green patinas of bronze idols;
let it wear thorns;

a marble sarcophagus chiseled of time
used as a watering trough by an Italian farmer
makes a museum of the mind
but if an American wished to be buried in a Cadillac
that would let it be even clearer
and less conceivable;
Sunday drivers are mystified by head-on collisions
        that condense time,

and the rituals of ambulances;
history becomes a pattern of clean-shaved euphemisms:

French immigrants who manufacture gunpowder
　　are sanctified by Jefferson;
young gangsters love and respect their parish priests;
all is safe; all like *Life* is true;

then let it pry jewels from altars
to ornament the bridles of palominos;
let it come down from effigies with ivory faces
and its blood disappear quickly from windshields;
let it turn wine into water.

To the Constituents of the Congress

> *...they are always guiltless...innocence is a kind of
> insanity...*
> 　　　　　　　　　　　　— Graham Greene

I was your honey and ash,
taught to prefer mattocks to mathematics;
I went to a state university
where mentally crippled children came, unable
to think, hardly able to feel, asking
　　to be rescued;
your bewilderment was my confusion;

in this there is no stopping;

matters were settled; unlikely gods alone
　　are strong and good;
real men are weak and sinful;
and you who inherited the fabled Christ
　　of mirage-following nomads

find in this there is no back-tracking;

theocrats and humanists called their country
out of a dying world to create new innocence—
"The Americans who instituted the monkey trial

        in Dayton
have alone proved consistent," Freud said;

convinced of your innocence, you
hear your allies accuse you
of vices invented by your enemies;

the liberated prove ungrateful
for their liberation,
the reconstructed
for their reconstruction;
the colonial peoples resent you;
driven by these provocations, you
plan to exert your power
to compel history
to conform to your illusions;

in this there is no relenting;

I was your violation,
your money and trash,
bought with Bibles and athletics,
taught to distrust poets and mathematicians;

in this there is no loving;

and unless you know that Jefferson was the first
and Forrestal the last American hero—
and understand the awful transition—
you cannot even know what question to ask
        to clarify you;

in this there is no wisdom.

Georgetown

May it please our unlikely saviors from the moment
        of their squandering blood
that we quietly here in Washington
listen at night to our friend, a Roman
by birth and faith, read Dante in the Italian;

may our pleasure seem innocent
        as thorns or a brood
of thieves breaking up before the sun
deafens a clear cruel bird, and tedium
clanks a veil of vending machines in the Pentagon;

earlier we had experienced a torment
        of Etruscan horses, loud
on Constitution Avenue, stone mane
breaking on necks torqued wildly, an intuition
of Marini's to unbridle time in the museum;

afterwards we passed a tamed cement
        percheron that stood
outside the Labor Department, in its line
nothing of running, and remembered the pain
of Pound at St. Elizabeth's and Perse in the Wardman;

and thought of Forrestal's flight from the ardent
        window to the sod
at Bethesda while the airport vane
cried clear weather east to the aluminum
bird, a wreath of brains rustling in its design.

Statuary Hall

The dancers, candled in their flames
cold on eyes and brittle hair,
cold on their marble shoulders, light
that is not pleasure but a way
to know by limits, and they know
time by decorum and love by art,
they find this way to imitate
the never final partially true—
they pray with dancing if they pray—
before the movement as they move
subsides to consciousness, before
the movement pauses as they take
this partial truth of movement and
believe pure energy is true

as if dead men were surely dead
because they move so little, as though
the deadness of ideas and men
is always carried slowly and
is true because this movement holds
the shaping deadness finally in;
they know that chaos, if they fail,
becomes a city, and if they move
falsely then all their partial truths
become a stammering of blood;
they move with courage, perilously
in plights of incense as they breath
freedoms tallowing coldly out.

GUARD OF HONOR

in memory
John Fitzgerald Kennedy
November 1963

West to Dallas

Leave the flattering libraries, the graceful Eastern towns
Leave the untold beads and the uncounted leaves of grass
Leave the blue panes of cathedrals, the red leather of law,
    the white silence of poetry
Take yourself to Texas in an open car
Be for one moment the advertised Zero of infantile people:
    rich boy in a big car, hair wild, teeth clean:
    young god without wound

West is the place to die It stands for death
No law except chance and impulse in that country:
    land blazing and sterile, cold with the howls
    of sun-crazed and moon-frozen animals
    with torn fur, then sun on the carcasses.
West is the place to die, my President

By day in a freeway
cavalcade of sunburnt limousines,
you ran the gauntlet of leather and lead
On the thin fabric of law between reason and chaos
you laid your head,
blood on the temple, then sound of a rifle
swaddled in oil
Hungry hands were waving
A black woman wept into her purse

Riderless Horse

From Andrews Field you ride into the Capital
A guard of honor escorts your sudden corpse
        down an aluminum ladder

Your widow stalks your body through an avenue
of bare sycamores, and one answering bell,
leading heads of state
        to altar and precipice

On the birthday of your son, your widow
walks bars of a dirge on the pavement
        toward fountain and abyss

Among swords of sunlight drawn by the spokes
        of the caisson
and the white manes of horses, she walks
        into noon and midnight

Above the muffled drums, the high voice
of a young soldier
tells the white horses how slow to go

before your widow and children, walking
behind the flag-anchored coffin—
and one riderless black horse dancing!

Widow

*and so she took a ring from her finger
and placed it in his hands*

Let her take his blood
     on her tongue,
his being wine
     at her green altar,
the sacrament of summer
     in her veins.
Heal her, her children
     with books and duties,
with winter land for walking,
     a child in her arms,
and no office
     except the natural care
of fall weeds bending,
     left, driven
And may she be
     fall, weeds, all
beauty's luck and fullness.
     Heal, make her well
with my country's bloom
     Let her have to know
     and not learn again

Supplication of the Poor

Bi-partisan committees of the Congress hail
     the hearse into Pennsylvania Avenue
Men in the Congress who were blinded by your vision
     and refused your living acts
pave the long route of your cortège
     with sanctimonious lies—
always the machinery for plunder and blood
     not yours then, or now—
the market rises and falls
Rich men pay no taxes
Lack-law rules
the substance is eaten

The husks drift in the wind
My President, where can we go?
Into what country
where the white-poor and the black-poor
do not have to barter dignity for bread?

The Post-Christian Era: An Oration

The witless prayers of children in the dark
        must ebb into silence
The eunuchs of Rome and New York
        must burn their robes
The violent and guilty boyhood of nations
        carrying rifles and crosses
must end and be forgotten

All the sacred emblems
        of religious awe, of tribal arrogance
        that have killed you
        must be laid down:
        the plowshares that were beaten into swords,
        the sacred wine-drops molded into bullets,
        the blinding cores of atoms
        that have killed you—
        all must be buried

The creation of gods to forgive
the evil in men,
the orgies of guilt and expiation,
must be left behind in the same way
men once shed the long hair from their bodies
and lost their fangs

Let them lay all their rings and weapons,
with their archaic beauty and terror,
on your grave

Light at Arlington

At Arlington the fall sunlight dies
Across the dark Potomac, Lincoln sits, hands on stone knees

At Arlington no steel or silver, no sword or chalice will remain
    clear as your eyes

President I love as my grandfather loved Lincoln,
in the silence after the bugle, lie down
Lie in your forest of stone
Lie close to Lincoln
On the dark hill a flower of light is blooming
    clear as your eyes were

PRESIDENT JOHNSON'S CHRISTMAS MESSAGE, 1967

My fellow Americans, on this day
Of great achievement amidst decay

In nations less fortunate than we,
Who are blessed by God, J. Edgar & me,

I just want you all to know
How your gov'ment intends this world to go.

Your gov'ment has informed Pope Paul
In the interests of peace, we never shall

Permit Asian fanatics of Mao & Budd
To shed an ounce of good Christian blood.

To Marshall Ky & his noble elite
We shall continya to offer the American teat

& Freedom's Forces in Saigon
Will back our pacification program.

For every ten children we napalm
A Green Beret will rescue one.

We shall persuade yella Gooks to be
Harmonious in drinking coffee, not tea,

A manly drink from peaceful Colombia
Where we support the reigning party.

& I assure you that in Guatemala
We want every peasant to drive an Impala.

In Mexico our good will is clear.
I speak Mexican & Lady Bird here

Spends half her time, those sacred hours,
Curing ringworm, eczema & the scours

Of little fat-lipped kids of unfortunate birth—
Or what else is democracy worth?

No need for Big Business to get queasy
About depletion. I rape easy.

It's not a game of hound & hares
For I love to reason with millionaires

& I quote this stirring slogan:
War is good business, Invest Your Son!

To give misguided DeGaulle his chance
We've surrendered our territories in France,

Legally ours by right of conquest,
But we think these good-will gestures are best.

To our Blacks in slums or behind the plow
We say, "You all be patient now."

And to make this patience stick
I've had Bobby & Abe chastise McKissick.

We must protect Democracy,
Not so much here as oversea.

And to the United Nations, Nu,
We have sent an honest Jew.

Some extremists complain of my daughter's looks
Well, she's a sight prettier than yella Gooks.

Harry Truman told them off that time
When they said Margaret couldn't sing!

All you mothers with tears in your eyes
Holding your Bibles, look to the skies,

See signs of our progress, Apollo & Nike,
& I may even send Senior Citizen Ike

To show the Chinese what a great old warrior
Can still do, without his gall bladder.

Of my Great Society the world will be heirs
& to shape it that way I'll need all your prayers.

But we shall go to any length.
The American mother is our strength.

BLACK BY WHITE

Health Education & Welfare Social Security &
Disability Office Leesburg, Florida

I thought she was stoned until I could see her eyes, then
I knew she was only quietly crazy, a black girl about 20
We stood in line together & whether I wanted to talk or not
    she settled that
What you name? Robert.   I be Wilhelmina
    & she took my hand in her fine hand, asked,
    You know what I had for breakfast, a glass of water
Her amber face tugged my attention
    like a fish on my line

She said at Sumter a doctor killed her first child
      by a forced abortion, but she had another
She said My baby girl be 3 months old She have no orange
      juice
She told me they had not eaten for 2 days now
People in line waiting for the office to open were staring
      at a white man & a black woman talking so much
These other Crackers avoided me, but how could I quit?
      Shit,
I've been hungry & will never get full   God, she was
      beautiful!
Still, I was surprised they let her out of Sumter Asylum to try
      to get work until I realized the attitude of the State
      was To Hell With This Black Girl
She said she will build a new life   O, yes! Until her eyes die
Her appeal for food for her & her infant daughter will go
under the office file of dead paper
As I leave, I lean over, touch her face & whisper
Make it, Momma, make it   Wilhelmina said, Mister Robert
      take care

I did not say: Blue Lady, let loose & die
for justice & mercy never were meant for you

Little Children

Little white children turn cartwheels & backflips on grass
Little black children perform them on asphalt & cement
      with an added twist

Alabama

to Martin Luther King

Come to the foot-killed grass, the rain-black shacks,
the porch rails solemn with flowers in rusted lard pails

Come to the varnished pine pulpits of ugly groaning churches,
to the beaten yards under China trees,
from cotton and sun on the blue bandannas of fieldhands,
their secret heads, their arm-frozen children like pineknots

and the crazy way of church singing, as if God were a hoarse frog
and hard times and broken bones were healed by a jazzy Jesus

And don't look lucky for being alive and hating white people
Come past the helmets and jowls of white troopers
your head bare to nightsticks   Walk your angry way,
drag an arrogant god to death between Selma and Montgomery,
die and be born—not on the road to Damascus

Free yourself from Christian violence and terror—
and from forgiving, the last white expectation and excuse
for little Sunday girls, so pretty! killed in Birmingham,
a *Bible* stolen by a servant in a white mansion
to teach a black man how to preach and pray whitely
O free yourself from gods that never lived!

Let your charity bloom only on the faces
of cane men and sorghum woman
no god ever helped or ever will
when they put bare feet to coffin end, are carried
in the hard song of a trumpet
to red clay no god has ever blessed

heard nigger to the last killed nigger,
said Sir too many times in dirty sorrow,
said God, as if that god had eyes and ears

For the Funeral of Malcolm X

> *As long as our civilization is essentially*
> *one of property, of fences, of exclusiveness,*
> *it will be mocked by delusions.*
> *Our riches will leave us sick…*
> — Ralph Waldo Emerson

Sellers, lovers of money, close your doors
On 125th Street bolt your shops
Merchants, count your money, and lock up
for a dead man who wouldn't turn tail
Collect no rent today from your slums

Kill no man in the names of your mothers
Take no payoffs from your numbered slaves
If one chair is sold, one lamp, one bed
they are broken on the floor of his house
If one wedding ring is sold, it denies
his love for wife and children

Are there any among you who know how it is
to live on slurs and sneers, chickenfoot, pigtail,
down to the last dime and the last bottle,
see the first cringe of a child at a rat's shadow,
with no place to go but to Hell and back?
Are there ten men among you who can still feel?
and lock cash registers under racks of knives,
blues records and phosphorescent shirts

Don't trade his corpse away like a dead dog

> Malcolm dead in tabloid print
> New York newspapers gloat:
> A *Black* Muslim is dead
> A goat, a bony fish, not truly human
> He had a criminal record, they said
>
> American Blacks are free to kill each other
> or drop firebombs on brown Buddhists in Asia
> But they must not threaten white Christians
> in the Archdiocese of New York

Tonight blue lamps shine in Harlem
on the stone-cold violent avenues
in precincts of the sparrow and rat
Over his coffin a liturgy of silence
from beaten men and women in random jails
from Michigan to Georgia
All over Hell and gone

On Miles' Tribute to Duke

The whole hell is honey my bees strayed to
Flown are the dark larks of Carolina
      & the wired-puppet starlings of Harlem

John Wayne said God went thataway
I never caught up with those horse's asses
I'm still mired down in Baldwin & Florida
I'm not the American who killed the rooster
        that prayed for rain at 4:00 a.m.
        in Black Town
        where bitten dogs weep at dawn

Let the owl scowl
Count wandering armadillos
Count wild berries & busted bicycles
Count dark children as they wince over hot sand to the honey
        of a church organ, drums & hungry voices
        calling to a microfilm Jesus in the brain

MINE SHAFT

Through an arbor of Laurel at the hole
the dead men being carried with blood & glass in their hair
their women mumbling in prayer

It would cost the company more per death
        to make the miners safe
        than to send a funeral wreath

Coal knows no rule
except United States Steel

SOUTH

to B. J. Parrott

        1.
I see water walk
I see children fly
I hear men and women plot

flowers finite in the bloom
I hear them speak a room
into madness into night
I hear the sick and lame
recite their lips and arms against
empty windows broken panes

Bankers, doctors, money to you
Priests, lawyers, justice to you
But black hands still hands
still eyes black house, hear
I see your dirty smiles
tractors aprons caps furrows
your guitars and green whiskey
I see your pencil marks
on brown paper lumber walls
Steal, lie, grovel, fawn
Take any iron that lies loose
any woman any ladder
Grin the bars that jail you now
Common, Common, O my father!
Common girls in tall white heels
over roadhouse gravel, boys
in white coats with red flowers
withering on your lapels!

I hear the crossed priest pray
and the prosecutor sneer
and the banker count his liens
and the doctor wash his hands
of us over our live bodies
over our thin coats and shoes.

2.

White, quit chicken
Black, quit lard
Needles, quit cotton
Whores, quit street

The sun falls down

The trees lean down
The birds fly down
The faces look down
Shadows climb down
My father dies alone
My mother lies down
The fires die down
Their breath's bright crown
dies down like bloom
this spring like dawn
on time, all time
Love in its light down
comes to its brief claim

Men, quit work
Women, quit church
Let the vines run
in the garden
Let the trees grow Let the cold
Christ quit breathing twice

    3.
Time stay love stay brain stay
I feel therefore I
stay where late we sing
We cause light to wheel day
heart-roar rib-silence
sun ice seed freeze
stolen fire early ash
We make injury pay the scar
I feel therefore am
flower post nail stone
I am love after love
I am buried without a harvest
due I am dying new
Brightness falls from the air
Girls have died drunk and young
O let the lamps burn
on tables bread wine music
Seed my brain into time

A growth of green ringed with hands
to protect your little veins
deep under the last freeze
Dust has closed your eye
I see therefore I
am sick and must die
Only lies are given me
Grass even lies to me
Earth tells me ripe lies
green against the fact of stone
Pity on us love in us terror in us
tears on us hands on us light in us
waste of us loss of us breath in us
pain in us growth of us light across us
Time's green last heard light.

4.

Timbers warp stones crack
Arms and hammers watch them fall
I have failed to build a house
artful quiet closed to none
where kind clocks smile at errors
mathematics makes of time
where the soil does not wash
women forget to be afraid
men forget the cold streams
of their children's unguessed minds

Make dark, my God, wreck
my walls and furrows! Let black
hover the marrow of my darlings
Prince? Poor man! You thought those leaves
were the banners of an exiled queen
with spotless hands, clear mind.

5.

Let loss let lack let stack
rake mow grain chaff
the last spectrum dust of us
Let the level mileward land

return the dust of handy eyes
harrow teeth rolled cuffs random straw
jay sparrow crow and star

Goodbye field stone river
Goodbye Legion Klan Baptist
Goodbye white virgin by willows
near a mudhole Goodbye Faulkner
Goodbye Elks and Eastern Star
Regulators Union deserters
Goodbye Davis Goodbye Lee
Goodbye evening yellow fireflies
mist of willow dancing ponies

Young father, who were you
Before your death, who were you?
Before you loved, who knew you?
Young mother, who were you
before your body burst and your
careful hands rescued my breath?
Young wife, who were you
before our child rotted in your
dear flesh, who were you?

God in the green of Heaven
imagined now, account to us
We are treated badly Pay us!
Give clods eyes Give us love
after good acts Give us back
wine for water knowing for seeing
Give us a law Lay the last straw
Give us full baskets to lay
at the base of the monument

Rack rifles Rack feathers Rack rue

FINCASTLE, VIRGINIA

Three lights burn
under the town;
three bells chime
auctions in the town;

children's voices call
to abdicating parents,
fatigued by pianos
and insistent Negroes;

Virginia is sold,
lock, stock and barrel,
the law libraries
spilled by teamsters;

three lights burn
the hooves under the horses,
the wheels under the iron rims,
the bells under the crosses.

HEADS UP

to Kenneth

Heads up to sight us, peach and honeysuckle swells
all over the twigs and rails,
corn grains in the teeth of loping rats
And us quick children in a summer of carbuncles,
all us rough cuts with berries blue
and blood on our mouths that call and call
     to the udders of German women

And at fall's last burning, gone small into wide snow,
     stalking a cedar, sneering at ice
We pissed on the same cold stone
And you, Little Boy, inside your far far fire

wore frost on your face like a beard

You knew as a child there's no mercy for poor

Grown sharp in our carnival minds, the axe at Christ's Mass,
the cedar so mute in its own scented crying
stood ceiling high, blistered with popcorn and red
      paper chains held by wheat-glue in our poor

Brother-man of our chained blood-brood of fond spawn
I have come to know blood when it dangers the State:
the cinders of Sunday black girls in a Birmingham church,
the corpses of white girls whose fear-wet flesh was a threat
      to the National Guard of Ohio:
(Malraux recalls that a holy man once came to Gandhi and said,
      "The gods are dying. Why?"
      "Because the gods can live only while they are beautiful. ")
O, brother dear, our gods lie faceless and quailed in cured blood
      in a country of no surprises
We have felt the visible blood leap from your broken mouth
      and my slashed forehead
pumped from us rough-cut horseshits, American ruffians
      who fucked the strange strangers and cupped our mean hands
      when the Eagle shit

And now in your face broken to kindness I see
smiles and caresses for all your tame darlings,
my own face now wreathing in this time of love
after wild and cruel sang away
and scars dimmed from red to blue

O, the years, years while the angel grew
on our Christmas tree!

And here it comes again like rain on Indiana,
on our way to an old barn waved with high hay
we stalked our impervious poor

And in the water of our dear father's grave,
      all his wet walking

sunk in a small mound of sand in Florida
And our dear mother wreathed in the wet of her
    grandchildren's kisses
Ah, her waning hands! O, say yes!
Brother-son, take my hand and say yes

For the poor, love grows round and fat on water

I nailed up a photograph of our parents standing
    in blind wedding clothes
before a small house circled by fodder
    and hens pecking rocks for craw grit

At home, home I lean beside a tree

They could not save our rainbows

Child rain knows there's no mercy

If I honey your hurts?

I've been stopped here some nights
l don't think the days are equal
This is a far cry
I sorrow into crops of nails, herds of stars, rains to the East run
My wrists ring with love's pulse
ls love legal tender?

Down in me, still rejoicing for our brutal innocence, still

There is this little I keep in trouble
That you shall know
That you may be
Only that you go

INDIANA

North from Louisville

The window blind is brown
in my window night
falls from a tower
holding a clock
across the river a city
glows, and beyond
fields of winter wheat
church spires and silos
bodies measure shadows
no words are heard

the rented room is quiet
the pingpong game in the hall
stopped at eleven;
the pale girls have gone
to the White Castle;
here silence is like
Dreiser dead, with a landlady
bent over his corpse
while her radio plays "Stardust"

I never draw the blind
whenever light comes
I do not want to miss it
light is my profession
it accustoms me to nights
when rats chew orange peels
in the wastecan near my desk,
and I stand at the window
where smoke from the flues
settles blue on the pane
the bridge looks handwritten
I draw my initials
the way you trace your identity
when you are not thinking

where my hand has rubbed,
light, not my name, comes through.

Harrodsburg: The Cemetery

The highway runs ahead of my injured eyes,
seeing only the concupiscent angels frozen:
the intuitive shame of motionless things,
the absence of consciousness and memory in the permanent grin
praise comes without honor, death without dignity;
the finite insult of prayers
takes no account of the distances
a live hand tapped electrically
in a red brick station against a green hill

an ingenuous painting might show a steam engine
        and gondolas paralleling a river
as on a pingpong table in a basement
a group of women suggests patience
while town clocks measure the distances
from railyard to courthouse to coal-bucketed kitchens

but nowhere is the recognition that love or grief can be real.

Indianapolis

The policeman's whistle is clear and thin
at the white island of monuments on Meridian
Street, weighted with tableaus of frontiersmen:
Clark in green bronze, sword drawn,
leans towards Vincennes, and pale green
water booms from the fountain
and settles to a stillness under the reign
of blue-and-gold state banners on aluminum
poles that face the tarnished Capitol dome
above six Corinthian pillars; the limestone
wilderness stretches, treeless, to the open
arcade of the bus terminal, a slam
of light down Market Street to the Harrison
Hotel, under a long red-and-white sign

gamblers with dry faces and sallow skin
ravel in the weaving walk of equal blacks with brown
expectations; the Circle Theater kills time
with a film based on a Lloyd C. Douglas novel shown
in Technicolor; and under his white helmet a modern
gladiator from North Vernon
creates Speed, a flying
red horse stenciled on the blue racer's engine,
while at the roller rink caryatids in
flesh-colored stockings support the roof, go nowhere in a din
of lucky wheels; on stage at the burlesque, near the wing
an Irish boy sings "Mandalay"; a bronze woman
with torch, on the monument's peak, faces south down Meridian.

Bloomington

The same way prayers end,
letters always begin:

Dear Myself,
                   Today
I heard music, drowned
in sunlight and slaughterhouse blood
and a strange sense of rubber
tires rolling around
the speedway without cars
or drivers, because tonight
after Hoagy Carmichael went back
to the piano in the gym
and Wendell Willkie returned
to the Law library
my father called me in
from a war to put on the earphones
and listen to Berlin
I had to listen then
because tomorrow everybody
would be in our attic,
my father's workshop,
to listen to the first
short-wave receiver in town
and hear the romantic music

of Central Europe as if
it were one inch away
in Berlin a band was playing
from under the workbench
the color-coded wires
sped into the world.

Milan

In the darkened houses
they watch television
Their walls are scrolled
with Christian mottoes in red wool

Coal piles by the railway
are dense and odorless

The county held the world's record
for corn yield per acre

Mechanical cornpickers stand like giraffes
Sheep make few night noises

Clocks are meaningless

Before a train arrives the switchblock
obeys a steel instinct for direction

No lives are suddenly sidetracked
Loss is criminal

A black standpipe wears
orange letters: STATE CHAMPS, 1954

Young cars ease to macadam
and accelerate with sexual squeals

The green glass of bottles
broken in the street

looks American

When Dreiser wrote he had no readers
When Willkie ran he got few votes

My cousin in bluejeans wept for Dean
and raced her Chevy the wrong way

down all the one-way streets
in search of ice cream

I did not suggest she go to a doctor
Who is insane?

Labels are dead wonders

Who is free? I had a gray jacket
too tight across the back

I strained against force,
my life confronted by perfect deadness

as I lifted the canvas mailbags
with brass padlocks, thrown from trains

I like to stand in the icy cones
of trains diminishing towards morning

It is not yet dawn
There is not enough light.

MONUMENT CIRCLE

for Lannis Thrasher

In cement leaves, with pigeons and rustling girls, the carved
                                        figures rumor
      deaf close histories;
this symmetry of white is your boyish hunger among cigar bands,

wine bottles and bare-headed warriors;
red, the instant affinity of my blood, dear cousin, for yours,
take as the first knowledge of what we are and sweetly ever were;
accept black, our tattered lingo for the long ambulance
that draws you, drugged, south from Indianapolis—
the wooden-spoked Buick you drove past Monument Circle to arrive
    at the hollow points of steel needles
doesn't count for much on a used car lot; the hypodermics taste
    the new sugar and the undried blood;
the final sweetness becomes as in photographs: all untearful
blasphemies whispered to sober daughter-wives standing
    awkwardly in the lobby of the veterans' hospital;

these figures, quiet in the fountain's rain,
this pride of monuments pities our limestone;
these stones at the meridian of our earth close us among
girls we were photographed with—a rural joke, this grinning
arm-linked stand with strangers, in our pockets the contraband
    of crimped bottle tops, sailors' caps, and the white husks
      of our pigpens;
the frozen pumps and empty buckets
are only relics of our inaudible childhood:
you with your black hat, baggy suit and determined scowl,
your tobacco-stained hands holding the trivial
    histories of Terre Haute and Evansville;

who, in my nightdreams, is as deprived as you?
who stands unslaked where the water shoots out from the fountain
    at the center of our dead city
over the graceless effigies of Union volunteers, where tongues of water
spew and curve down their glittering acclaims to your dry pity,
as in my nightmares, you?
forgive my staring at you unaware, my terror
of the photograph shot beside the polished car, the back door
    you will abruptly enter;

in Monument Circle at night cornet and tambourine play;
you have left me under the weight of charitable coins, so heavy!
how can I, in your absence,
hear them sing, and see

the white faces of secret girls and the stone lunge of history across
     their knees, the broken columns,
without remembering your noon grin, its dimestore permanence?

there you are with your smile, clear body;
there you are with your invisible landscapes
     rolled under night;
you illumine with your silence and star-faced curiosity
the heavy slaughterhouses south of the reeking city;
you clarify for an instant the tumult of switch-engines
     at crossings,
tall boys running in gymnasiums, and the capture of girls;
between the quiet paralysis of statuary and the quick thirst of stone
you retrace our country
where the blue windows of stonemills shine through black thickets
     and sudden patches of snow;

I am surprised by a green gourd's ripening
though I recall our overweening gardens, the heavy berries;
I remain alive to pantomime your dawns
over ration cans and toxic sleeps,
     the earth binding you;
I crave deep minerals, living always, and the bright increment
     of furrows that curl my ankles;
I want the life that gave me this holy flesh, this form, this keen
     plow to carve out brisk sunflowers and onions,
this torment;

O the fruit breaks our speckled trees down!
and time's brown scrawl on the fields sure of weeds' fast colors
                                        in fall
traces winter to window;
I want the life of your hand-me-down flesh
before the boy stirs at last
the deepest of all vegetal memories
and the bayonet follows his entreating wounds;

slow tides of brown blood barter existence for forgetting;
I invent the long days of our curious and questing indolence;
people stream about me in little black cars;

military caps sail brightly away;
on this holiday of my words and my dreaming
the tones of many voices on forgetful porches,
and leaves, brown and pious, affront your quiet acre
where wreaths of wired flowers stare
and crossed rifles shoot briefly;

concerning the slow echoes, the warm grass with its yellow
        worn distances—these turn
by the endless car windows to a perfect horizon,
and in the spade-gashed abyss between being and forgetting
the grave discovers what has been given to it;
you lie whole; wounds heal; fastenings roll from you.

SHENANDOAH

Before I began I had all there is
Now I don't know where
I go & smell like a wet shot
I call myself & preen
I know how long it takes meat to rot
I crave & don't spare

I'm what my father whipped with whips
I'm what my mother wept for keeps
I'm my brother's nails
because I eat with my fingers
in front of his blue-eyed children
Sister suffers me for kindness

If a man thought he was understood
he's a fool & should suffer
If he thought he was loved
the flash came quick & I wasn't there long
in Shenandoah's soft dale
The sad girl with wise eyes—
how dense was her body when it found its way?
Lie out, still   Surround grass in blue city fists

and long swayback hunger!
I pool in her nerves, swig & shine
Yes is the muscle of the blind flower
Yes opens the mouth of the dreamer
Yes is tart & suck of laughter
I woke & saw cold light
on the tight sills of her skin
under the vines of blue hills, red apples
O, the cunning leaves, the chill grapes!
I see why Jackson
rode round the Union

I sway here   It's my time.
I stay anyplace over
The courthouse clock in Winchester
told my crimes to the Greyhound riders
I looked around but saw no blood
I'm blind as a sitting duck
I came here in a bad sleep
I bought up my arms for salvage
in the junkyard of Roanoke

I wanted to tell about
but got sidetracked
I'm what anyone would call
when I remember my given name

In the rack of a cattle truck
calves scratch my hands with little tongues
I make my own music
I catch a hatful of whispers like old rain
that will not fall as long as I

SLUMGULLION

O, my World City, where young black men slammed me
      down under the silence of bystanders on the granite curb
      & took money plus a few kicks in the ribs for interest earned!

My head bled, yet I knew savagery before the kids that beat
      me were born
& it was all green & burning in a meadow when Saxons
      ran me down
& threw blows hard enough to spring piss
I guess I knew batter & barter of flesh when my grandfather
      took his knife & scraped my arm & said
That's part of you, Son
I saw my dead skin

O, I phoned ambulances for passed-out bums & saw
      the rants of Hell's Kitchen crisscross a street
      under the patient eyes of cats
& heard in open windows the love-sucking of heavy breasts
      where a kiss leaves a red welt

The lonely morning   No dreams move
The stingy wind down Second Avenue is over
Pregnant women parade their bellies to fish markets
The priest is only a man   He knows nothing
At dawn a painful moon dies over Brooklyn
Italians on Cobble Hill shit & pray
Saint Patrick's Cathedral spires dream like flowers

QUEENS PLAZA

to CFB

*And yet, suppose some evening I forgot
the fare and transfer...*
        — Hart Crane

1.
The small trees in Queens
on the way to the neighborhood
church where the ikons
of Christ are painted red,

grow in small round plots
in fields of cement;

I saw a thin girl
at a bank of white candles
whose flames were the leaves
of her burnt childhood
and their smoke was the scented
cry of her dreams
in a chapel of plaster hands;

as we went to my place
in Brooklyn Heights
she talked about her dead father
and her mother, living alone,
in a brick apartment building
with five roofs over her head;

when the fog closed down
the harbor and Brooklyn
near dawn I listened
to the foghorns while she slept,
then quickly her frightened eyes
strung on telephone wires
until she found me beside her;

to Chinatown and the Village,
we stood at the front window
of the train to see
the tracks curve down
into the 4th Street station,
and did not try to guess
which way the bending laughter
would run ahead, or confess
the terror running behind;

her face is clear always;
I love its shape; I see
her mouth move inaudibly
under mine with love.

2.

When the train screams
at the rails' flange
coming into Queens
under the neon signs
of Blackjack and Dentyne
chewing-gum, and the smell
of bakeries is strong,
I cannot remember
whether to change—change
for what station?
my mind cannot arrange
the free transfer;
change must be
only an illusion;

in March cold rain
falls in the city
and taxis make white
tracks from Manhattan
out to Queens, going
from the stone office buildings
to the brick apartments
where sycamores and umbrellas
shine in the neon
of bars and newsstands
with pieces of iron
laid on the wet papers
where the subways end
and the rain walkers
wiping their glasses
enter and exit,
their raincoats dripping
on the platforms
where we stood in the cold
many times together
waiting for a train.

NYC

There now is your insular city ... commerce surrounds it
with her surf ... look at the crowds of water-gazers there.
— Herman Melville

1

Gray to the marrow, pale as tall smoke
across the East River
the boneyard of Queens burns

Into my window charred letters fall
from the grim incinerators,
some still legible, with lovers' initials

and the brown reek of fire

2

Pools of blue children under the haze
under the sailing hats of nuns

3

Private darkness strays into rubble
where the Catholic god and the Jewish god
grow weak stems in cinders

Terror is private
A woman is murdered in 38 windows

Everybody is nobody's keeper
Ask mercy of stray cats

The dim roar of traffic over bridged boroughs
comes savage and sad

4

On an island staked out by stolen car aerials
professional liars in glass canyons cross
Madison Avenue and disappear
in secret Connecticut

Marcantonio's city of shattered wine bottles
and brown cut flesh rings Columbia in

In the midnight streets I hear
young whores cursing

5
The smiling girl who committed suicide,
mistress of gem thieves, hid a black eye
under polaroid glasses

She screamed the length of her lover's coffin
She rode in a Cadillac long as a whore's dream

Lover, tell me the best hate
Murderer, tell me the best love

6
The cold wind shines

A train clicks quietly under the iron grating
where, with axle-grease on a lead sinker,
a coatless man fishes for lost coins

I watch raw-knuckled care for all trivial, all small
And here

7
Banks whisper money
Male whores reply
Oiled locks slide free

8
Aluminum trucks bleat like lambs,
hauling barrels, crates over the cobbles
Streets grow long with vegetables and messengers

Near dawn I walk among fishnets and boatloads of coffins

And where the streets move, treeless,
I hear pawnshop trumpets

    9

The ferry rides under gulls crying
in high monotones the water's given names
over Crane's forgotten bones

And wrecks passed without sound of bells

Acropolis builders, stand with me here, see how you failed!

POET TO PAINTER

My poet! he said
Now he is dead

Arthur Sappé could see lyric color
in an eyesore

His first outdoor show
in the Village, watercolors hooked on a row

of black iron spikes
before Judson Church

We belittled the guys
who bought buckeyes

hardly noticed his rainbow labor, heart's own,
purchased none

Back to West 26th Street,
the old slum, the reeking night

Five flights up from the garbage can
I followed soft inspiration

To the surf off Staten Island
with a saw & a gallon of wine

to cut driftwood for sculptures, grain
to hack, polish & form

Now hand melted, heart burned
& ashes thrown

on the gull-slanted domain
of Hart Crane's Brooklyn

water. Artist, I send
my death-greeting past that bend

where wounded men share
duty to quality in a mock civilization

purblind to rare vision
That beauty may wear
the brightness of despair

WIND FROM NEW ENGLAND

I'll not have rats
I keep snakes
The well is clear

I go by the rule
of sticks & stones
I live on the edge
Down can't matter
Scars grin at the sun

I'm here, hide & hair
among watery roots that wave
their white entrails
single & slim

All here green as fire
I'm in the place where snakes
leave their scrolls
Before day can break
I wave the sun up
& call the birds here
to festoon our sunflowers

I lean on a fence
evening while white stones fly
over the pines, then the moon
tracking wind down
New England Freeway
Taconic & New York Thruway
Sawmill River Parkway
past November granite
your sleek hearse
ribboned with ice
& you in the iron ground
eyes melted that spelled my name

Pretty snakes lie by the fire
under your crucifix
The water is clear
There are no rats at the door
where I shouldered you up
like a sack of potatoes

HIS GONE DREAM

Float, Robert, float your boyhood dream of a fertile land
        of sweet democratic society & love
O, it bends like a rainbow to no end
Your magnificent America has been up for grabs
        too many times
& floats now on a sea of chemicals & oil
where late the sweet birds sang

The great cities where you wandered, giddy
        with beauty
are Prison Compounds, patrolled by troops
        in crash helmets

So the scheme of alcohol to kill you
        will in a hospital tag your great toe,
        eternal son, sad child
Yet you will dive under & remember a wild
        bank of ferns

ABOVE A TRAPPIST MONASTERY

A hand taking food beyond silence through an iron door
        glitters with fish scales;
beyond these purities thin sleet squeezes life from lambs
        in a hard winter;

in this world of wool and horns, my fathers,
tobacco leaves in blue cuffs, lean to fevered children;
and a young woman behind a coal bucket, hands in her ringed lap,
        dreams clear madonnas,
in her womb a new dead child;

fathers, be quiet, devoted, weave careful shawls
        for Clovis;
hide time in history;
in your silences
existence stands darkly before being;
in your renunciations
be not only clear but radiant
at the grated window, the shut door;
contain the furious germ;
pray that you kill no one;

from your city of mathematical lines,
full of varieties, successions, contrivances,
look at the lewd friezes of my vegetation;

inside the black sunflower stalk see the stillborn child;

when ice dripping to the flagstones uncovers
small bird skulls in your stone eaves,
look at my carrion land where winter lambs melt like hailstones
and be awed; curse and forgive the dead passion; absolve
this clay that takes no apocryphal wings!

fathers, during your daring and incredible silences
    I speak on,
washing your houses when you turn to dream;

though I did not attend her funeral,
I saw her many nights in shallow sleep;

I fished among ferns, eons of leaves, carp skeletons
    in limestone;
I sent her from the earth only all the leaves, lambs' hooves
    and fossils of children who cry killing

CEREMONIES (IV)

LAST LIGHT

Love is the last light spoken.

— Dylan Thomas

Snowfall

Snow falls in Transylvania, night falls, your eyes approach
under trees by the fountain carved in winter light,
corolla of your quick face, creature, fugitive
Snow falls into the fountain, white flower of your face
I left it to my mouth, host of my tongue, my blood
My ribs listen to your veins running with the small sounds
trees make at night when they break into spring's early light

Near Dawn

You that I love
who lay with me
I give to you
this injured dawn
the night confession
your veins dream
book and ring
hands ingrained
praise of money
good fortune of books
music, engraving
of my mind on air,
sadness of windows,
the gladly dead,

you, visitor
to the long city
of my arms,

your unlocked hair
the new grave
of my mouth, my words,
as I sit beside
the sleeping faces
of your bent knees

traveler beyond
perfume, bandages,
denials, epitaphs,
terror of midnights,
you waded snow
over brave grass
in a park of bronze
statues of innocence
and speechless murder
to the safety of
my knowing ribs,
your promised eyes
morning and fountains

Near My Destroyed House

Near us the sun falls
on this cold street
Wind from the river
wings high stranded cables
of green signal lights
Yellow trucks haul
stone houses away,
their careful foundations
uprooted by iron

In sunlight and cold wind
we go by the glass stores
blind with the long glare
of counterfeit Christmas
On velvet I buy you
a thin smiling trinket
to engrave with my name
deep in your new wrist

Red lights in the towers
of radio stations
fall on the pavement
near us at night
close to policemen
and Army stores

On gingerly boardwalks
we pass excavations
where rusted ivy
and frozen marigolds
clot the iron teeth
of shovels and draglines
where the blind houses
fall in the perfection
of new careful snow

Below bells and music
harshly electric
we go in the freedom
of gold rings and locked hands
under the steel cranes
and blue arcs of welders
among the destruction
of old houses

On still roofs the snow heaps
our endless inheritance
of answerless questions,
crackup and rubble
of minds by machines

And my house a shell
where I lead you and stop
before the vine tatters
and look where our pigeons
have flown the green gutters
and folded their feathers
below the stonefall

Clear Place Near Time

Hold my sight
Look through my eyes
Be light
  Surprise
my hands with a green
paper fish that scales
our good fortune
For your birthday wish
you me Know
the crippled way
we have to go
If priests pray quietly
this morning, we must fall
into an older cathedral
     and be
quiet in this garden Touch new
my morning eyes
  Surprise
my face with the spectrum
between your fingers, the chimes
of light as we fall
O, wing me your burning
arms, your let blood running
into my hollow side
caved for you each creation
of earth and the flood
of light that greens your turning
body to its birth
free of all crimes!
Stake your criminal pulse
to the close compass
of my wrist Hold nothing true
but your goodness and beauty
In a blue guess
riddle our innocence

Sleep of Triumph

Now to the stairs

above this *Vacant* sign—
the sign predicts a place
where I may live, at low rent,
provided I live alone,
sober and quiet.
Lying is part of it:
a woman at her door
asks me about
my religion, my habits,
and I tell her
I am conservative.

I did not tell how you
left fur slippers, card decks,
half-eaten apples, how you
deviled our bright nights
with whispers and
the small avatars only
your fingers spell,
how you took
my arms round you and
how certain we were,
our looking was,
our knowing was,
your blue blind eyes were,
your blue seen known eyes were,
your blue still brain was
our sleep of triumph

Easter Sunday

Now and the way runs
here and away
into the cold trees'
labor with white buds
Into my land now
we have come this way
Steeples and tombstones
dial sun away
Into my country
I carry your hands now
in our known way

Into this cold field
clever in weeds' ways
rabbits and colts run
close and away
Over my land now
they run away

I hear high crows
all feather bone hunger
cry over the field now
up the next hill
and disappear
Fled is that music

Now and our time is
now and the time
Here our first way was
knowing without lies
Now brittle seeds doze
Land plows crows
lift their frost iron eyes
now and away rise

Now winter bodies lose
honey and mercy, choose
rain and the rusted hoes
of my lost boy's days
All that I love dies
quick as your tongue cries
up graves in turning trees
harvesting birdcries

And who believes
a young god lies
with healed wounds
close to green flies
cold-souled and risen, grieves.

Running, It Never Runs from Us Away

I am your heart's inaudible beating you cannot speed or slow,
my clay your clock, my face your map, my pride your flag
a mirage of love's red, and with white stars unseen before you
as you walk from bars to suburban houses with men
who cannot hear my voice in your opened mouth
or feel my fingerprints on your pressed hands.

LOVE,
THOU,
AT ONCE

CINDERS

to Wade Donahoe

*…what business has the poor face of the man
who officiates as poet? None but to disappear,
to vanish and to become a pure nameless voice
breathing into the air the words…*
                                     — José Ortega y Gasset

Figure

to R. B.

The blue guard in the museum
stands quietly behind the crystal of his watch
I do not care what time of day it is   what day
but look past the back of a woman's head
into a triptych set against the wall's mosaic
the wings folded on brass hinges slightly
forward like a sleeping bird's

She is waiting for me to speak
but I do not know how any longer
I have forgot what vowels are so sacred
she must not hear them

I do not know any longer
whether the speaking would be
to the full face, or right or left profile
She might be the central point seized in some god's beak
or the parabola of all wing-deafened women

I do not even think any longer
what communication might be   I know only
that the young woman requires drama
two voices in monotonous strophe and antistrophe
two bodiless voices recalling dreamily
something performed in a place
of no dimensions   by persons without blood

Where the oblong medulla tapers
to a May Apple root coursing down her back
the vowels are only electricity   a pulsing
formless   secure   Nothing is going to happen
It is not as if I tossed pebbles at a lucid skull
high up where a light burns for my darkness
The head of the woman is turned away

I wish my voice may be lost finally
in her contemplation of sound
My voice must carry nothing to vary
the currents of her sentience
The speaking is only to beat pure oblivion
on her ear's three delicate bones

No place unwinds murmur and color
beasts listening   people walking about in clothing

To speak is to lean forward and enter emptiness.

Mirror

> *As silent as a mirror is believed*
> *Realities plunge in silence by...*
>
> — Hart Crane

I have made something I will not remember
very long   I have made only this sign
These words that gesture to me are not important
I do not mean them   If I meant,
the words would seem to express things
that I am in continuous possession of
This is impossible to the mirrored world
Silvered and carboned, the mirror is cold and thin
Nothing it ever was stirs within it
Nothing is presented to it that was not otherwise
Glass is the will of fire, disinheriting all
the fire had signed and crossed with a leap

I do not want to say again
I have seen a world of wool and oboes
so long as the river runs softly against the shores
of my voice
or that it not wake the woman who sleeps there
This would be singing   But who would believe
desire can always mean singing?   My words say nothing
other than they might themselves be

Rocks   wheels   idiots—
That there was no subject, ever
I did not care
at the time of seeing
when I thought the sand
is burning   the air is melting
and numberless gusts of fire
create the mirror: all knowledge, all being
That there is no subject   and finally
nothing has been said does not matter
That line and form do not exist is enough

I do not even know
how what is said differs from what goes unsaid
what orders of the flesh deployed in mirrors
have been surprised in attitudes of perfection
what oceans of sound crawl under the skin of silence
The world lies uncreated   The makers die
at some point near the beginning

I stand in the white halcyons of undiscovered worlds
whose creatures are too surprised to fly away
as in the sudden gaze of a mirror
one has no time to turn away
from the first image, the one always believed
Turning requires another surface
The silver dust of a mirror is thin and clear

One act is all one mirror can endure.

Nothing

In this first year of Nothing's being
the hour the iron clock strikes
and blue pigeons and tan pigeons
fan the air to flame
and return to jell on rotten cornices
separate   glowing with the anguish of distinctness
it seems that I should not have tried to join
unlike things
that relations which appear substantial are always false—
That the sun will rise tomorrow and end the sleep of lovers?
If I refuse to believe the sun will rise?—
Even if everything we wished were to happen
this would only be chance   random motion
purified of any meaning
For this reason
I do not make words I might have made
for a man and a woman

That would have been before the bathing of pure Absence
the nativity of Nothing
and its being wrapped in white cloth
before the pigeons lofted their loud grieving
when I might have made a harmony
of unlike things in the likeness of a word
of hard and durable alloy for the oneness
of a man and a woman

But it is not there when I speak
It is Nothing   That is only its name
This is not to know the thing but the name only
This is to know Nothing
This is to give myself away freely
and to represent my humanity
by a stage-direction
for which no play will be written

A world of the happy is another from a world of the unhappy
This is only to say death has always been

that death is not an event of life that changes
that death is not lived through
that death is not an experience

That in this death worlds do not change but end.

Drum

Have circuses for the living
and the dead who are so noticeably not moving
that you heap earth on   or burn
but have also a parade for the dead
who fill the tents and television rooms
or walk in plate-glass canyons
looking as if they were alive   Some of them
are at this moment applauding red-and-white clowns
Some are weighing their bodies on public scales
in which they drop a penny to see their good fortune
Others hold your face between their hands
and cast gregarious shadows
as they step through the heads of drums
and emerge in an arena of gold sawdust

If a group of people arrive talking and singing
have them step through the drum
The zebra deaths   accept them   Discover
that emotion is not obscene
even when completely surprised:
A frightened man is dying
with impatience to see if God is
A girl pulls long white days from a stem
counting: he loves me, he loves me not

Begin the parade with a herd of zebras
See the wayward whimsical gait
of creatures that go unshod   Remember
that the ultimate reality is a circle of animals
who do not live only to develop lines in their faces
Laughter is serious
                              If young men set fire
to the tent hasten them through the drum

to find themselves in the dressing room of the aerialist
where they can see her as she would be
splashed by a fireman's hose or dipped in a barrel
to see her clear thighs standing among reeds
far from the arena

If you will follow zebras with clowns
to go along the curb pinching the bright faces
of the dead   not incorruptible   then have
drums beat a measure for walking
the long walking in lines that lead nowhere
There is always a dream of perfect chaos
A dream of fire is what a circus is for
What else could so have lifted their faces
out of dreariness?   Recall
that among certain ancient peoples
it was believed if their minds were lost they were dead
though they laughed and ate and drank
and surely thought
the ash that bound their ecstasy was real

And when their bodies at their lengths unfold in silence
if they are black from charring do not loathe them

Watch them   See how quick they change!

Alto

The man at the piano in Harlem
drinking a mixture of beer and white wine
is playing "After Hours" by Erskine Hawkins
and remembering the Deuces of New Orleans
A black river flows from Barbados
through the gullet of an alto man

So that nobody can look in
the windows are painted green
The rudimentary eyes of radios
are green and narrowed in the dark walls
under arbors of telegraph wires

while the eyes stare
and the time-signal chimes
in outlying centers of impulsive loss

The dying agitation of a pebble dropped in a pool

Such parliaments we hear in a back alley
Young lords with multiple tongues
clucking in subtle rapport
Behind green windows burgeoning of horns
in the register of noon
Through green windows they ride out in turn
Lords with reed-sweet mouths and crows' hands

The yolk of a bird's egg broken on his head
a naked child walks about a village
his steps uncertain, his balance precarious
walking a dusty road between mullein stalks
and cucumber vines   He hears
the bull-roarer, the sacred flutes
sees the masks and the magic ouangas
Sometimes the child sees a white face
that hangs for a moment like mistletoe
in halls of doubtful ancestry   Sometimes
walking in the sparrowed lane he gasps
at a white statue with outstretched hands
His mind richer in orchestration then
draws a purple skin over a green grape
that coasts the risen currents of summer
winey where the heat clings
to the underside of leaves when the sun is softest

On the Gold Coast of Florida
the moon rides south to winter   and
round a coral hotel a frieze of persons
carved hastily, ill-shaped, gregarious
tell each other over cocktails
how Biscayne Bay glimmers in blind windows

entertain us   what if it's only smoke   only air?
that's for the time being   that too goes down

The lies blow trivial as the leaves of potted palms
entertain us   but that's for the time

Now it is after hours   In his mind
a clay road runs through South Carolina in August
after the cotton-picking
when fishermen doze at the creeks
and deep-bodied women in cabins
putter with beeswax, dried fruits, beans
The child recalls resinous cat-faces
slashed on the turpentine pines
He is afraid to take his lunch to school
Grease spots on the brown bag stare at him
He remembers a sweet-sour taste in his teeth
He pauses to adjust the reed of the saxophone
instrument of his birth delivered
with bloody cord still folded round him

entertain us   reach us
across rail yards and nightmares of ingots, Manhattan,
a violence unsubdued by music,
the tall gray island
reflecting the gasoline flares burning
in New Jersey
we will pay you

The men on drums and piano
wait for the alto man
The moon was yellow
The chanted *go* of voices
disturbs a school of minnows in his veins
Now his only thought is how high the moon is
above his ducktails preened with vaseline
and crossed where they tail off deep in the river marsh
He lies an inch above the water's skin
held by whole monotonies of tone
When he listens he hears always the same tone
Song of a redwinged bird in the audio
Now we have to go
Now we have to go.

HILL ABOVE BEDFORD

Carved stones legend us humans and dwarfed on this hill
where the serious dead, divine in their ugliness, lie;
snail-horned stones drink the rain quietly,
and we who have felt the thirst of minerals and the hunger
    of animals at dusk
resign ourselves to contemplation of the holy perfection
    of ugliness;

what is beautiful is completely human,
and a stone is not a thing to plant
unless hard wishes have worn away
and nothing is left but love;

our fathers' land is poor, the timber second-growth;
all their tall illusions are cut down;
their walls are broken by cries of foxes and crickets;
and we who cannot build because we must sing in summer,
our minds made intricate by the sickness of music,
have these stones to stare down vanity;

here moments cannot stay, but fall trophies away
    like the wings of dinosaurs;
we cannot enter these stones, placed at the center
    of chance and innocence,
only a white monotone of instants that belong
    to life, and its quick going;
dressed fit to kill, we walk on this hill,
    Cain among the gravestones;
here pain moves leisurely, and cannot be put by;

serene in their ugliness, our fathers' uncharmed clocks,
with precise indifference to our humanity, are silent;
dressed in black cloth, satin round the arm,
we walk all afternoon, lame and beautiful,
knowing these bones and flowers we carry perish
    and shall not come again;

in a cedar tree, chants of young doves resume
     as we pass;
the fence rails are black, the burdocks green
under the blowing rain of spring; we listen.

LINES IN PRAISE OF MYSELF

My passion, drawn from me, bitter and rich

My gall in an era of chronic humility

My candor that stares in grief at my country
     while a pious Texan makes war on small nations

My refusal of false gods while others write essays
     and plays about saints

My laughter at Mary, my mother, my wife
     while Paul prefers abortions to condoms

My simple denial of the lies of my parents
     while others build self-abasing psychologies

     * * * * *

My love of children and candles while
     churchmen set up No Trespassing signs

My favor of poor while government offers
     dollars for pride

My awe of rivers and columns of stone,
     the visions of builders:
     David, Cyrus, Jefferson, Mao

     * * * * *

My incontinence to the celibates

My land-drift to grit-city

Nothing saves honor but to be
    assassin of lies

EMPIRE

The Red and the Black

after Frederic Thursz, his painting

Dark is a pageant of descending color
in light's sudden absence,
indistinct as water is in water;

in the shadow of French valor,
in the after-image of chance
the death-mask of Napoleon hardens in plaster;

since the torch is out, melted into air,
the remembrance
of its final red is torture;

so it must be: now only black can vesper
the once
bright blood, and all is done with wonder;
the sound of march music in the streets passes over
and unifies Paris,
then goes, and in the Mediterranean vision of a painter
the city's windows close endlessly on the somber
darkness
and the artifice of gardens becomes clear.

Empire

Churchill, Eden   breakfast, newsprint   calm, storm
and so it goes with political movements:
scaffolds, irons, carried to the West country
was the flowing dialectic of the Saxons:
before shields, arrows   after, the loud slipstream

If they live long enough to complete the adventure
it will run towards the morose river of word-of-mouth:
a cone of words fast to the mouth of a young captain
light-headed at seeing so many men dead in the China tree
loved by the wind it cannot help touching
the wind to his eyes dazed by his prurient vision

In London the bishop gives a slight tap on the cheek
to the child dressed in white
who received the body and blood of his Lord

In Africa mudchildren harden and are glazed brown
and the clay birds they make with famished hands
take life   they fly over the cathedral
drawing the marriage hearse by ribbons in their beaks

while green Malaya, green China
turn slowly under their breasts the lice-gray eggs
for the white child's Easter.

Star

for Frederic Thursz

All day, higher than the heads of executioners,
the earth rose against the clean blades of bulldozers
and fell without echo at dusk on galaxies of bones:
the seedless bodies of bearded men, milkless women,
children with dark stars sewn on remnant clothing;
in the leaf-green country surrounding Dachau the discoverers
climbed down from the iron of their machines
and smoked on the raw mounds, mouth deep in bones

At the end of history
these
were discovered dead:
a victory
over starvelings whose knees
bled;
the beauty of the head
and eyes
of a fly or a Jew, something to be
crushed and buried
at the beginning of history

On the iron crosses, on the claws of black eagles,
on the cold edges of the voices of young men,
on the shields of tanks and weapons carriers,
on the Bronze Age swastikas, on the tenons of oak tables
of knights in their tarnished lust married to violence,
on the Druid trees in wolf-toothed swamps, on wire cutters,
they were caught on the crosses, dismembered and killed

In the darkest night stars grow.
Black threatens them, always.
Some are clotted with red.
Some drift in the incandescence of the sky.
Some are goblets lifted, held for a moment
in a strange land

On Leaving the Tower of London

High on the hog of Normans by Roman ruins
brutal as Virginians after Appomattax
who trailed across the Mississippi
to kill settlers, rape their women & laugh
As Normans butchered Harold's Saxons
& dyed England's rivers red

In this white tower liquid lead
was poured down the throats of queens
& Raleigh bled
followed by a barbecue that leads to Texas

Mercy ought to be a luxury of power
yet the body of Anne Boleyn
head severed while Henry played tennis
was thrown unshrouded, uncoffined
below the flagstone of the chapel
where late I stood

From the Roman wall, reinforced by William, to Wren's
Magnus Martyr is the distance from
the Red Dog to the Last Chance in Houston

It's only a cranny of time from London to here
where Oil Overlords swill bourbon, abuse women,
slice pigs & fly

Under a Florida Palm

Stevens: "We say God & the imagination are one."
Hazel: "Imagination is one minus God."

Yes, Wallace, seas are splendid
Yet this is not Key West
Order died with you
Ideas, the very marrow of your carnal magnificence,
        are colorless
There are no cockatoos

A still lake near Orlando
        where a young widow coaxes her waddler over sand
        the boy puts feet into delighted water
        his head is a sweet melon crammed with seeds
        of the father he never saw or put infant arms to
        the widow stands thin in the white uniform of a nurse
        who draws spare blood from strangers

Grown dark, she is the pure profile of all orphans
        unloved, spun to sudden reverie in a nick of time
The dusk slant of her, Wallace, would remind you
        of a savage queen & the terrible pencil
        you hied a Cochin to
        that baton, that ordered change from

delible beauty when she took her husband
by the hair of his head
in tight tumbled hilarity

to this green dark
this figurine embalmed
in my breast
not from Persia, Egypt or Key West

Recital

for Lauren Sylvester

After the beautiful gods Osiris & Jesus died, there is little
        left to admire
except pouting breasts on a Florida beach to remind me of all
        goddesses
when Sidon & Tyre & Smyrna swelled with incense

& a mad kid with razor slashes on his unwilling jaw
& a florid friend with white hair standing on the beach
        like a heron
& an American Flag shooting the breeze above a hotdog
        stand

When then from this strand of dead crustaceans & harsh
        ocean light shrill as an elemental cry
I made my way inland to a little place with soft air through
        colored windows
the glow centered on a piano & a music stand where a tall
        girl
stood in a long wine gown & long brown hair
        to play a flute

then across my closed eyes paraded a marble frieze
        of Isis & Helen & Ceres
in sturdy notes
like muscles running on the flanks of goats

LETTER TO THE KENTUCKIAN

to Wendell Berry

1.

My earth announced by rising flocks of leaves
Under green a horse's veins strut on his running
Sunflowers bend east   Their tongues take summer's host
In the morning mist apple buds flare like candles

Here comes the sun to my magnet!   Too much life!
I have bitten my mouth   I spit blood

In my mouth more than thirst for my own blood and the blood
        of other animals,
the holy mass of summer! yes
and I pray by waving a scythe at high grass

In one long rush of my breath
a dandelion's white head
bursts to tufted life

Fly, little wild birds! Handsome cock fathers, sing!

At the end of cut weeds and battered clods
        the kiss of water
        stigmata of sun-fired windows
        echo of walls
        silence of photographs
        patience of drowsing flowers

Fireflies light their day   Cells settle   Sugar seeps
I hear the scrolls of corn stop unwinding
        and the birds stop reading them,
        tuck head under wing

I have my own twiggy dreams—
To town where carnival birds
        fly on whistling sticks

Weave a circle round me

I'm dizzy   I'm lucky   I'm magic!

And I can step in any river twice

    2.
Your hard hurt bring me   your unread books your wrong
eye-glasses your illegible letters your relief checks used car
payments your hard hurt hearts bring me   your death insurance
bring me faceless documents printed in code dealt you for inked Xs
and usury   your hard hurt times bring me   your bruised hands
porkfed weakness green vomited mornings your lardassed lovelings
bring me your dry faces dry gardens dry batter your dull senses
your hick brains your helpless hands your slat backs having bent
over your already done work bring me your grinning brown tobacco
mouths your loud laughter you fools! you fools before bankers and
sheriffs O weak weak and hurt hard by your dires hurt blue and
so sadly go inferior clumping into general stores go rummaging
in black back pockets for dimes among bent nails and twine go
let the townsmen take the dangling buttons off your Sunday coats
pluck lint from the chains of old slow watches and other
poor white and black bone and metal cold now in their
candied town hands

    3.
Crossing the Ohio
where my homeland breaks at the river
to an orchard of tombstones
beside the superhighway
where engines sing in anger
under a neon frieze
of hamburger and beer stands
I have come to gentle you, Old Ones
to soothe you like colts with my hands
carry whispers like wheat to your corpses

Old Ones, honor me now
Your bones decorate my wrists

Dead children swindle my arms
In the exile of recall
From the hourglass full of spiders
return me your sweet hearts

Yes, Mother, your pulse sobs
over a hip-carried child
Father, your serious eyes!
Yes, look me straight in the face

Dead blood turns black
Grief is a way to turn
But who can see tears in the rain?
I gaze at your flowers of lime
I call these stones by your names

4.
White scales the house   The painter is dead
Green binds the house   The trimmer is dead
Hands search the house   The lovers are dead

5.
A gone world, ours   Once upon a time

Our chronic dirt, hick curiosity, boys' blood,
our hands cut to the quick
bled like the sawed-off horns of cattle
from sharp tools our fathers thrust into our ribs
before we were old enough to shave

Learning was pain
during the first terror and failure
But what elation to discover
we could pinch, pry, jimmy, jack
a world into place!

After we knew sunsets
fierce as the severed head of a horse,
washed the crusted blood from our foreheads,
took pleasure no longer in killing,

learned how to smile at wives and children
and nod our willing heads to hairy sod,
dream smooth dreams,
not shouting fear and rage,
learned not to attack the already wounded,
but kiss eyes, hair, faces of sufferers
and care for all suddenly young and torn

What meaning now? Virtues?
Repeat Colonial tales of common acts and faith?
Green people, green rivers?
Devoted builders, defiant to kings for sake of us,
bringing fire to our hearths?

Who, if we shouted, would hear us in the drive-in theater?
We have seen used-car bumpers welded into sculpture

WHEN THE GRAY SUN

When the gray sun undone in the ash of my eyes
    in an eclipse of love
shall rise on the fair air of my breath
    to lick my heart like Shelley's
Say I surmise there are holes in the universe
    dark as my entrails & the sundown lark song
I have been near tears for earned sorrow each tomorrow
    of no mercy to the bundle of my unslaked bones
    wound in binder twine

CAROLINA

Leave Taking

I am kissed away by sober women, those saltless good women
Goodbye to the air-conditioned car that carries Mother & Sister
    in white Sunday hats and gloves
    south to Florida,
riding thigh to thigh in the ambulance of optimism

When you go away, Mother, Sister,
in your long desolate car with radio loud and trunk full
        of beans, corn and Bibles,
Alone here, I study minnows and toads prettier than words
The creeks ask me silence to hear in
        below the thunder of moles
My arms are wet with our Father-Husband's ferns
My cup spills over with leaves
I train them up the trellis of my windpipe
I laugh their browning edges green again!
I whistle back to our dear dead Father's birds
        here on this hill

Noon of goodbye, and where? The engine of a tractor
        mowing far away sings hornet songs

To My Loved Woman

First wind of fall tonight, a fire in the hearth,
my father's stuffed birds on the mantel, rain, hail,
then a sky so cruelly clear that the North Star rang like iron
I curse nothing, not even the wasps that sting me
l look, l listen, I love
I rattle with unstrung nerves freely with dying weeds
My arbor is swollen with grapes that will slowly ripen
Each evening I walk out to see their gradual blue
I sit on my mountain under a full sky
I am empty of hate, free of illusion
Real deaths stare back at me, not just the imaginary
deaths of gods that breed religion and philosophy
I hear the loud teeth of a dog, ripping
first the brown hair then the thin blue hide of a groundhog,
now the chill gnaw of gristle, loud in the human hall
I have cut through that meat and was stopped at the bone
Destruction, the squander of continents, the gunning down.
in Asian meadows and American cities, of brown men and women
Blood is the crown of my race   How good of my father
to have killed only himself! He kept Christ's thorn

Wanwood Leafmeal Lie

The mist drops slowly, Father, falling in
The wood is ricked, maple and oak, in dry
Your birds sing heavily this fall, your sunflowers in
In the night mist heavy animals go   They sink in
The earth under the grape arbor is rich
as your caving face
and the frail bones of your hands, yellowing in
Potatoes and onions sweat your cellar in sweet
But the grapes, Father, the heavy clusters gather!
much happier than a Christmas tree   O, Father, you
lying therein, you rotting too   Dear Man,
I have cleaned our hoes and rakes and hung them in
to dry   I have told you our happiness
and why   Father, I am willing to die

WAITING FOR THOMAS WOLFE

for Louis D. Rubin, Jr.

Had I been splendid, either good or evil
equal to tragedy, as you were, the man I follow
this season of ripe grapes & dead children
of our cold mountains, it would have been
I was a spring of love nobody drank—
for my reck, gamble the long run away
for the brief ecstatic & the green
nose-thumbing flag of my disposition

Come Hell or high water, I care for
    the timid women
    slanted like asparagus in Carolina
& sweated men leaning on fences in tobacco country
others propped on clean elbows in city libraries
& in Asheville a broken figurine puking
    her first white whiskey

Where? What? Have I lived only to discover
Shakespeare dying eight years after
      Milton was born
two years after Newton saw light
nine years after Spinoza was born
five years before Rembrandt?

Is it to find the electric Golf Cart
rather than the Statue of Liberty?

Is it my father, a physicist, in a bathroom
finding out he was merely a higher animal?
(Mozart said he made music the way a hog pisses)

Is it to hear Lincoln at Gettysburg declare
"That government of the rich, by the rich & for the rich
shall not perish from the Earth"?

Money spits the electric sky of lower Manhattan
By the shores of Brooklyn I sat weeping
while the tall Tarheel, drunk & lost
on Montague, babbled for sirloins

This is me welling froth to love my mouth
telling frost to arm the acorns
for poor hands, lip sores, to gum the suckers
of the mountains, their old magic:

Presto Chango Buttermilk & Bones
The Cat Bit Off The Pump Handle
& The Kittens Drowned
Flies In The Buttermilk, Skip To—

Going to the Fair in St. Louis
a mother, a child & his brother
the engine rolling along the Wabash River
& over Indiana the high & sorrowful skies

When in the dawn of an end, a fury warp, a child choke
a sorrow sturdy as a casket

a boy lost by his given name forever
in lonely mortal time
& we were cursed, Thomas, to tell ourselves
cured & rotten as October!

There is a footprint in darkness
A bell strikes twelve
& the flying year is gone
My life is water that has shot under the mill
It turns no wheel

YOUNG MEN, YOUNG WOMEN

for Nancy MacDonald

In these Christ-hurt born-damned days
to tell you my truth would be criminal, to say would be
first I love you as I hate myself for my false life
of tempered lies to your unhardened skulls, is
to walk away, after seeing you in sunlight, to my dark house
in these deaf and dumb days, and to tell you

No, it is not this
No, it is not that
No, it is not even the other
It is not May Day or Christmas or Passover
It is not like anything you have ever thought

It is not even grass near water near trees, and
is not the incredible skill of your knees and fingers, and
is not the timeless stare of your young clear eyes, and
it is not history or drama of Oedipus, Jesus or Lear, and
it is not rhythmic, as in making love, but

it is more like sickness, if you are alone, and
it is no honor, no honesty, and it is
bad education, bad politics, bad art, and it is
the way a child is at birth and an old man at death, and

It is the face you see on my face

SUMMERTIME

At daybreak the other
men & I gather
We throw hay over
the shoulder
At noon we make over
the children & eat & drink beer
& check the bailer

At night we pour water
all over our skin & lie down
Then terror
an Austrian doctor
said would be there
is there

CONSIDER THE LILIES

No clock strikes for a happy man.

— a proverb

1
How can I praise dandelions enough?
Even my tame azaleas amaze me

September cut down my father like a weed
He toiled not
Neither did he spin

2
Because these trees cannot walk
I wait for the Carolina moon
to stalk them before I shine
high as a white pine

A herd of trees cowed by a storm
I feel worms slide under the leaves to drink

A storm is what it wills
Leaves battered down
before the agreed rainbow

When it rains I take credit
I struck the rock

3
Shadows are friends
They know I hate the sun
for its injuries to me

Dreams hold night
The moon sheds pumice
into my eyes

Under a scythe-moon
deer & rabbits gnaw apples
under my midnight trees

The moon said: Look
at the cornfield
Silks rent sugar

Smooth in, little breeze
Time my skin
Crust my ears with pollen

4
A sweet small woman
slices peaches on a copper tray
Nobody will go hungry

My woman sucks the meat of artichokes
in olive oil & smells antiquity now

Maybe the wind will run away
Maybe it will be Sunday
& she shine like a fish

She laid leaves over the rotted spot
on my soul, succulent lips like aloe

At night she groins me
in a red house
Owls call softly
The parchment of our lives tears
& suddenly we are

Inside the womb
love will start
The embryo hears a heart

After you left
I held death by my hindered hand

Only fantasies tell us we loved

5

Here are sparrow nests
like rag dolls, so ugly
the straw falls beautifully out

The birds I hear sing
are dragons with wings & lice

A cardinal & his wife,
shavings of scarlet,
stitch twigs in a cedar
for two eggs

Opening his egg, my 3-yr-old cried,
"Daddy, it's the sun!"
Suffer the little children
I remind myself:
Before they die children
grow deeper than you

6

At dawn the cock's wattles
rhyme hens to huddle under
his yellow spurs

Violets anointed by dew play blue
I walk out into me

Eave water sorrows down
Dilated tulips tell the time
The implant of a dead star
in my bad eye

My white Leghorns fly down
at wheat time
I draw with fat kernels
the Christ star
& my birds form it
I draw David's star
& they form it
In a barnlot I create
from craw hunger
patterns of history I ken

7

Dreams are my perpetual terror
The dog rushes
I cannot move
to beat his skull
with an axe handle

A dog ran beside me
black like the space
between heart & spleen
Only by his dance I knew him
& chill overbare

Until I woke in terror
the dog had snarled
& circled in

8

I welcome all night sounds:
peeper frogs, alligator bellows,
limpkin shrieks, owls singing
courtship so softly who,
the strum of the banjo legs
of the wheewhiddlers

I hear these instinct cries
far from the terror of us,
us unable
& at dawn I draw in the hooked
blue catfish

Down on my hunkers below a sycamore
I hear a half-grown loud bird
demand insects
No matter how many times I salt
the birds' tails & pet them
I am ignored, I am nothing

At dawn lily lips speak
to the sun, their master
Today I cannot kill
Yellow is life's color

9

Ospreys scream then dive
like magnets for little fish

My legs break the tide
I tug the moon to Ireland

Waves lift & lower
Christ is my albatross

10

The cluttered cat chatters
her gleeful teeth at sight
of a robin on the lawn

I've seen animals shudder inside & out
while being slaughtered
I hear cattle low far as India

    11
A death-bound moth touches
one antenna with the other
closing the circuit to light

A moth eats my wool
Should I read history?

    12
I know no concepts
only bodies palpable to last touch
It is not being I understand
I suffered a haunt
in a clay graveyard

You fall far before
you open your eyes
to what you have dreamed
all your life
Before this moment
you were immortal

    13
This stasis is memory
My knowledge of evil
is murder & suicide
going out & coming in
I have been shot at outside
Inside I have been cornered
in futile rage like Bacon's dog

What I hear by the sound
of my voice makes me tremble
for evil I have sprung

I speak no matter
only form a vortex
of joy for my voice
in chance to happen

14
I have no repining thoughts
that I deserve a better life
The sun gives me cancer & showers
& flowers & a stomach for fish
So, fat & sassy, I wear out nightmares
realer than waking hints of crazy

An orange light burns on water
What of the dark in my eyes?

Night has no dark for me
for all, all is darkness
in which I see

The more death I enclose within me
The more alive I become

15
Like an oyster its pearl
sanity hugs the insane
& singing to the mindless me
welcome without heed
sloth, terror, joy
as my heart chimes the hour
without knowing the year
Let me grovel in praise
in the basilica of my dreaming blood

DEATH FLOWERS ARE

Death flowers are growing on my arms
I don't know where I am
I don't know where my hands are

Their lustrous purple blooms grow longer
than childhood's fertile blight
when sunlight tormented my face
to bring ill

Once begun, it cannot be stopped

My flowers fan tall on wrists, their fragrance
        welcome
as the odor of powder from a fired gun

RESEMBLE

How people look cunningly alike—
I see them years & cities apart
Yesterday, a schoolyard ago,
a yellow-headed girl looked
like a photo of the one I loved
ten years ago

If I had thought about this very long
I'd not have wept that long
or lost my way in a labyrinth of eyes
that stare me down in dream-time
equal to the beauty of this one
going walking

NEAR TROY

In isolation from others
my store of humanity dwindles

Maybe a wretched childhood
listless from hunger

deprives me of humility
& makes me sulk in my tent

& lets me unload my shotgun
& weep for every Helen

Yet a subtle bond
connects us marked for pain

Much water flows underground
that does not well up in springs

SOFT COAL

> *Cover her face; mine eyes dazzle. She died young.*
> — John Webster

I

Soft coal of morning on the county courthouse
    stone & wood houses down by the railyard
    black as pain & the all-night diner below the hotel
    serving rubbery eggs to the drunk trainmen
the snort of steam pistons, the throat of a trainbell
    tolling your short time
the cluck of the mower & fragrant grass under
    wash on the lines before sun of black morning

You pulling on black cotton bloomers
    & a skirt of flowers, my dimpled darling,
    to walk to highschool
    & me, your worshiper, a hungry fox tracking
    solemnly fearful to lose sight of you

Frost melting on the blades of the mower
    & Monday wash dripping from stiff scarecrows
    to arms & legs limp in black sun

II

FDR closed the banks & my father & friends
  retired rifles & shotguns
As Dillinger sped thru Indiana to visit his mother
  on Mothers Day
police hid in the basement of the black courthouse
I stood on the curb of Rt. 37 as his black Ford V-8
  blasted by at 80
I held my arms high to greet my hero
Did he wave back or do I imagine?

III

Who taught the shy boy to smile?
Who held his head when he puked his first chew of
  long-green?
Who bent to him when the limestone fell & staunched his
  blood with her hair?
Who taught him what his tongue was for?
Who pressed her mouth to a leaf of his Bible
  & left carmine lipstick on The Songs of Solomon?

Little Teacher, were that blessed time endless!

IV

The handsome husband you wed at 16 in a black stone nave
first raped you then ate then spat in your food
then circled your waist & pressed out your breath
  until you turned blue
then drenched you with liquor like a mare
then set you up in a room above the train tracks
  on a coiled spring cot where for $2.00
drunk trainmen rode down your numb body,
  not blood, but gin in your veins

V

Unto us a sign is given: Death
Down into your whore down dead stitchless body
The sun excluded you
blessed by my wept innocence

We shall not find again the limestone quarry water
        of our sleek green joy
Death, yes, Death, yes, Death, yes!

VI

Sunrise on the black stone statues' chiseled faces
        black churches, little black stone stores
        where the girl went carrying

The sun wanders down to get a drink of water

I carved with my knife your initials & glorious bold hearts
        in the bleeding skins of sycamores

VII (homage to Paul Celan)

Black rain of morning, I drink you, I drink & drink
There's a girl with unspent hair in a funeral parlor
When she leavened my tongue it became
        alive to seal & say
all words I've ever been given of the broken human
These words are a wreath on a casket
There's a dead girl who loved me   Black rain is drinking
Black rain is drinking my eyes
There's a dead girl's hair lies over
        dreams that tear my body
        from bed in terror of semen

Black rain falls over the town

HOW IT FEELS

I could say how it feels bereft of friends loved
This is dangerous because I could honor death utterly
I could throw away dice & cards & the Complete Shakspere
This is dangerous because I could forget pain's amnesty
I could tear up photos of women whose faces are the braille of weary
& discard tintypes of men with hard eyes who nested me
        on their black vests

I could become a sad child again & parade my hunger like a string of
    sunfish
This is dangerous because dark might smother the seedbed
& I'd forget to hate the crow & the cutworm that flies in the night

I could even think it's important to stay alive
I could forget to throw this away

SPECTRUM & SANDSTONE

to *Harriet Sappé*

Pale sky   Pale turf   Pale horse
Albert Ryder

Dead fish   Dead ferns   Dead talons
Morris Graves

Sandstone worn   Granules drifting   Cold animal
Flannigan

Rain on Chelsea   Rain on pigeons   Rainbow
Arthur Sappé

ISLAMORADA

to *Frances Whyatt*

Don't need love
Need alcohol
Don't need touch
Need alcohol
Into alcohol
Never pour water
Water weakens
whoever you care
Don't need love

Love asks what it lacks
in the bars of next
Froth of the Keys
like tiaras on rocks
The white brine of gillnets
The tang of dead fish
Awash the shrill light
Fandango of palms
& my pure pilgrim
jumps coral after
Like a bird drifting
coos to her soul

Come back, come back

FOR THE FIRST DAY OF BENJAMIN

In the amniotic seas
where great sperm lured
Milton & Melville
a green bottle drifted
a note inside with your name

Your memorized gills dried
& suddenly trees for your eyes!
Dry land your fortune & curse
In the early dew of leaves
birds wave & dry their wings

A friend of your parents said:
I have doubt about bringing a child
into the world at this time
May this verse erase his innocence

All times are evil
from the first stone thrown
to the high-blown atom
glorifying Eden

In Japanese atom
is Original Child
Was life made safe
for Caesar or Gandhi?

"I see men as trees walking"
Below an angel wreathed
in chiseled stone laurel
I see a bird recline
& a woman slice an apple
& your arms, your reaching arms!
She hears the parlance of your body

The music of a truck horn
& headlights bloom
on the moon's blind side

CLOCK OF CLAY

Be this as I may
     thirsty, red-eyed, fresh out of honey,
     pitiful & wrong
     a liar & tonguer of puke
I cannot think about what I am thinking
     or know what I'm knowing next
I did not think this out
It came to me all of a sudden
     like the scream of a whore being beaten in Ironton
Became a rager
Became rotten by faith in hymens
Fouled oven, green spewed potatoes,
     green dotted crusts in the breadbox,
     lumps of mold in the grape jelly jar,

To revive from death each morning
     with a sexual urge defying this latest suicide
& see the schefflera plant kicked over
     soil inextricable from the carpet
Aspirin reminds me my friend has cancer

& yet God has not said a word
       even though this is Sunday
Melon rinds on the kitchen floor
Magnificent cockroaches with amber wings
       scurry for hideouts
my head does not throb for conscience
I insulted nobody

I begin to live subterranean
       downy with sick wishes
Hurry to hang up the phone on pretty New Yorkers,
       friends dear & nervous who have never pissed on grass
Voice of my body speaks in high tones of disease
Many sweetnesses will go down with me that were never spoken
       & nobody else could or ever will
Delicate willings will die on my fruitful hands
There will be no trellis in the garden of my bones
       to train them up to sun
I send these to you undone
I have been the hermit bee of all sweetness

I have no future   The river
       is flowing backwards
My past is my present
& I retort to Charcot, Freud, Husserl
       Binswanger, Heidegger, Buber
       You tone-deaf piano tuners
       who wanted me to become what I never wanted to be!
I am becoming nothing

Melancholy & fear of heights are part of becoming
I have that sense of being crushed, bones & muscle

I am the man who cannot exceed himself
Threnody is my name

Who is the doctor?
Who is the patient?

Now I echo the shadow that I am

Losses chain me & I'm stuck in the mud,
    the dirt of death on my hands
& the world shrinks to my cowboy sombrero
    when I was green as an ideal twig,
when I sang while milking cows & flooded cats' pink mouths
    with white comets from lavish teats
I am only a reed, the weakest reed in nature
    but I am a thinking reed

Things break away like brown tendrils
    down a lattice of roses
Stand under the spire
Christ isn't there
    only a dead Jew my people pray to

By praying to a dead god you have insulted me
Let not any god nor human law diminish me
The spire holds against hell & is beautiful
    all the way from Roma to Constantinople
Everything falls away
    down a trellis of brown roses
Take this poultice of hope, these fat green leaves
    off my eyes!
& the spiraling red veins of the embryo
O, galaxy of life that bears
    the bronze stars of dead light!

Hungry as a child, leave a pie on the sill
    & I'll eat it & lie about it
    if I get whipped equal to what dies inside me
    If you grew up poor, there is nothing like
        a bean sandwich or sucking a raw egg in the barnloft

The dirty earth hides me
The sane man ditches around his house like Noah
But my god turned out to be a eunuch
    on a throne of wax
When lightning struck, the little god melted down
    along with candles & buttermilk
We searched for the blind kittens under the porch
    only to kill them with a kind hammer

Sycamores drink the Wabash of Dresser, Dreiser, Porter,
        Skelton & Carmichael, true

What am I made of?
The sweet water of limestone Indiana
The weight of rain, snow, sleet, mud & manure
Very well, how do you smell me,
my colleagues in universities?
I shall put white pockets on white trousers
        & die of Lucky Strikes
        before you discover

Mosquitoes don't fly in rain
        so I can bait my hooks for blue catfish
New River girl, the glossy boys tailing
        didn't find you
I'd give up my front seat in hell
        to teach you how to make love

I'm at the bottom of the barrel:
        feet infected, blood sugar high, no energy
        legs so weak I couldn't take a bale of hay
        from a pissant
Nur wer die Sehnsucht kennt
However, beloved brother,
as we go down, as we turn down
        to a lettered stone
as we go down
Drink up   Drink up!

Little boons swarm my face
to probe for blood & leave itch
        & experienced spiders leave a red spot
        on my pillow
        to remind me who's boss

I run a treadmill
level with evil—no gain into good
Experience is no help
I must do it all over

Now is the time of night sweats
      && wakeful despair
far from playing football & drinking milk
      instead of alcohol
My head rims into the helmet
      dented & scarred by wishes of heroism

I hear the click of a Japanese camera
      on Keats' sedges

The High-Rafter-Bat politician said
at the convention they had hippies, gays & way-out people
They had some long-haired sonofabitch singing
      The Star Spangled Banner
      & he was so drunk he didn't even know the words
      He must have been some smartass Liberal
His wife reminded him:
      You don't even know who Willie Nelson is

The leather glans penis dangles
The blue frog lashes in a fly

Once I circled with my arms
      orchards, groves & vineyards
I was rich with pure lust
      for all clods, shoots & sprouts
Now I am only a grain of dust
I have been to a strange land
      & met the dark man

My mother was a virgin bride
& I'm her first son, her prince
But I'm the stupidest man ever
      in my veins running carousals
On the human train I'm the caboose
Even God could not set a dove on my head

Great-Uncle Bob's house in Jennings, Florida,
had no screens against mosquitoes
where he died insane

I'm named for him   Bless me, for you could not sin
He was called like Isaiah to dispute the priests of Baal
Having no oxen to lay upon a pyre, he shot rabbits,
laid them upon chestnut rails & prayed mightily
No fire came from heaven
Betrayed by God, undone
He walked from Indiana to Florida
He lived on yams & peanuts from a small garden
until, caved in, he happily invaded hell

After the priest told her she was wed
the little girl in her hippie tattered long white dress
& barefoot came down all the aisles
& hugged us each one by one honestly
That child's heart was surely placed

In the final direction of the elementary town
        spartan children of Appalachia advance
        whipped & bed-wetting
With my axe they crack the multicolored dome
        of a terrapin
They kick dogs & yank the tails of cats
        until they spit
They eat raw turnips, suck eggs & smoke Camels

The last shall never be first
Beaten from birth, they will shudder
        in the leather straps of an electric chair
Clouds wind over small grim houses
They shudder in high near fear of tornadoes
Even cats are afraid to kill, their first joy gone

Sores, eruptions, melanomas, burnt flesh
        & a surgeon saying I am to buy back my life
        if I give up the inhalation of blue smoke

My life has been lived at night
        in the chemistry of dark slavery
Before my life is reinvented by tubes
        in imitation of the living cord
I shall cut free

After you do the first thing
the second thing is go down to the water

I have come to hate my life
        revealed in nightmares
        schizophrenic by night
        in the handcuffs of language by day
Often the damned know without being taught
I swear on a family Bible whose binding
        is the hide of a redskin
In a way destruction is happy because everything
        seems the same
Man in his maggot warren insists nothing is wrong
as long as there is ice cream & an emperor

Often I lie down & dream
or take the revenge of sweethearts
        who went next, simple

It would be arrogance to think I could lose anything
My memory is so poor that it is always losing & finding
        the same haunts

To stand up, you have to be able to fall down

I'm alone & glad of it
A time comes when a man gets shut of himself

Priestly & hollow I stand on this ground
of names from England & Germany
I sit on a throne of straw
heaped up by raw men & women
        with wrinkles like iron filings

Know, Thou
        the arterial fertile trails red as a cock's comb
        on a ridge of sycamores
Know, Thou
        the evenings of lovely lust

Know, Thou
     Hinder no heart its wash & weave red sluice
Love, Thou, at once
Love, Thou, excessively

Clock of clay
I sit by the seacoast of Bohemia
Sturdy beyond belief, white marbles
     lie to linger forever
Under the seal's wide spindrift gaze
Silurian stones dream of eyeless peace

FOR EPHRAIM

Now a life is lifted from eons of water, fern & bone into the arms of
     East Instinct & West Light

I rejoice! Your birth swims love's blood

May the butterfly wind you in sunbright
May you never be caught in a riflescope
May ideology follow biology
Ideas will surface later to confuse you forever
May you learn skills as axiom, as your fathers advanced with wood spears
     toward their totemic brothers
May the owl, whose wings make no whisper, drop a torn squirrel at your
     feet to teach you how still death is
"We cannot prevent the birds of sorrow from flying over our heads, but
     we can prevent them from building nests in our hair"
May you be an adventurous boy who dives into cold Easter water to
     retrieve the Cross, so to make material your soul even as the young
     god was made flesh
May you leap & hop & be scratched & bleed & be patched up & be
     stung by a bee, for pain is the measure of joy

As you grow, may the odor of sweating girls obsess you
As you drift in the maelstrom of being, may a cold light burn to
     illumine you

PARAGRAPH

Beside New River I walked alone & sat on a boulder
& let my feet fall into the rapid water. My mind
began to sway away. I sensed a creature near & saw
a new-dead deer by the lone rock, its hindlegs in
the white froth current waving like a metronome.
I felt no shock. It was a time before thought was
invented to measure years, days, hours—no tick
of the human. Before religions, before any space
between life & death. In my quiet breath I was
some thing that simply was—without meaning,
the deer, the water, the sky, me before I became
myself. I thought nothing. Everything was for granted:
water into sky, deer into water, flesh on rock.

CEREMONIES (V)

CELEBRATION ABOVE SUMMER

Hear dark the priestly insects of my endless summer coast down to cells
    of wax,
and kind weeds bend my flowers to their colors' end;
in my thin acres hear time burn stones deaf
and radium's fine ticking to my flaunted ironweeds' blooms
stop in amazement at rough measures, twined of handclasps
and the rule of hammer-bruised thumb;

                    wonder and stature
of young celebrations shot from the dark earth build silent
my endless prism of rusted axes and fruit jars glowing with fireflies;
and curled in the quiet speculation of clods, my black calf,
sweet and voluminous, hooves maggoty in stiff air, columns high
the buzzards sailing;

                   O see my land turn back,
my summer ponds waved with cattle, my ironweed candelabra burning,
my knotted chickens, sure claws austerely clamped and dawn-triggered
to sweet August branches, sap-crested, wild and immune;
O hear my crony leaves measure fine spaces, inviting
    the brisk moon-stares
to shout out clear reeks under green flies, beautiful calf!
your magnificence sickens me with love;

see my slat gates nailed back to the green yawn
    of grass; see, under sour water,
mosaics of mint, and my country run
back everywhere green, green.

AFTERWORD

IN EDITING THIS collection, now and then I asked myself—or, to be honest, Robert's ghost: What Would Robert Do? If anything, the ghost gave a smile and a shrug.

The first editorial decision was whether to follow the order of previously published collections, with sections called "Poems: 1951–1961," "American Elegies," etc. I quickly ditched that idea, not to tie this life's collection to periods in that life. I avoided a biographical chronology as well. However, the burning intimacy of Robert Hazel's work, especially the poems about women, and Robert's deep sense of place and of his milieu, inevitably form a biographical thread.

The sections gather poems loosely based on themes that, as I see it, carry through Robert's entire corpus of work. I'll leave it at that; it seems best to allow "who touches this" to discover (or ignore) what those themes might be.

The placement of five poems under the heading "Ceremonies," each introducing each section, is an editorial indulgence; those poems are among my favorites. And although Robert could act pretty undignified at times, not so deep down he possessed all the dignity of an officiant of life in our complicated, chaotic American cathedral of cityscapes, farmland, small towns, churches; heroes and myths, people we see in passing and sometimes stop to know, family, friends, and lovers.

ACKNOWLEDGMENTS

These poems were first / previously published in:

American Poetry Review
The Centennial Review
Choice
Dark Unsleeping Land
Deep Summer
Equal Time
Esquire
New York Quarterly
Goosetree Press
Hika
The Hopkins Review
Minnesota Review
The Nation
Of Poetry and Power
Poetry Magazine
Poetry Northwest
The Provincial
Prairie Schooner
Southern Poetry Review

And in:
Poems 1951–1961 (Morehead State University Press, 1968)
American Elegies (North Dakota State University Press, 1968)
Who Touches This (Countryman Press, 1980)
Soft Coal (Countryman Press, 1985)
Clock of Clay (Louisiana State University Press, 1992)